THE
COMPLETE BOOK
OF
RIBBON EMBROIDERY

THE
COMPLETE BOOK
OF
RIBBON EMBROIDERY

HEATHER JOYNES

Kangaroo Press

Acknowledgments

My grateful thanks to Kath Chate, Effie Mitrofanis, Beatrice Russell, Nerylla Taunton and the Embroiderers' Guild of New South Wales for their contribution to this book and especially to Doris Waltho and my husband Jack for their much appreciated help and encouragement.

Heather Joynes 1992

Unless otherwise stated, the embroideries, photographs and diagrams are all the work of the author.

Cover: Basket of Flowers by Heather Joynes (see page 100)
Frontispiece: Detail of floral cushion by Kath Chate (see page 104)

Reprinted 1994
First published in 1992 by Kangaroo Press Pty Ltd
3 Whitehall Road Kenthurst NSW 2156 Australia
P.O. Box 6125 Dural Delivery Centre NSW 2158
Typeset by G.T. Setters Pty Limited
Printed in Hong Kong by Colorcraft Ltd

ISBN 0 86417 482 9

CONTENTS

INTRODUCTION

Embroidery with ribbons has been in fashion at intervals since the eighteenth century. One has only to look at eighteenth century portraits of the aristocracy and the well-to-do to see the extravagant use of ribbons in costumes for both men and women. Ribbon bows, rosettes and ruching abound on bodices, stomachers, robings, sleeves, hats and shoes.

Actual embroidery with fine silk ribbons seems to have been confined to small items such as stomachers, workbags, pocketbooks and pincushions. Many of these were worked by amateur needlewomen as well as professionals. The ribbons were narrow, only 2 or 3 mm wide, and often shaded, the colours being woven into the ribbon. Chenille, fine silk gauze and floss silk thread were combined with the ribbons in delicate floral designs.

The pad for a sewing box (*circa* 1800) is typical of the ribbon embroidery of the period. The pad covered the elegant mother-of-pearl sewing tools in the box, and is made of satin. The colours of the embroidery are bright and the design of a basket of flowers is a favourite motif of the period. The stitches are very simple, straight stitches in shaded ribbon forming circular flowers, buds and leaves. The chenille is couched and there are straight stitches in floss silk on stems and leaves, and French knots at the centres of the small flowers. The large roses have been made of gauze, cut, folded and gathered into petals. This design with its pretty border would make a delightful picture to adapt to ribbon embroidery today.

From the 1820s to the 1840s ribbon embroidery appeared on men's waistcoats, on reticules, needlecases, pincushions and other domestic items. The pincushion from the middle of the nineteenth century has a wreath of flowers embroidered in straight stitches in shaded blue ribbon. The centres of the flowers are satin stitched in floss silk, and French knots are scattered around. Bunches of ribbon loops decorate each corner.

Pad for a sewing box,
circa 1800. Collection of
Nerylla Taunton

Pincushion, *circa* 1850.
Author's collection

From about the same period is the black satin drawstring bag, embroidered with a floral design in chenille, narrow shaded ribbons, gauze and floss silk. The small spray of fuchsias is especially charming. Again the stitches are simple: straight, satin and stem stitch.

At the end of the nineteenth century, ribbon embroidery again became very popular, continuing so until World War I. The striking picture of chrysanthemums is probably from this period. They are worked on black velvet and signed 'Vera' in paint at the lower right hand side. The ribbon used is a soft rayon in a cream colour, and the embroidery was painted after it was worked to achieve the beautiful shaded colours. Each petal has been formed by twisting the ribbon before drawing it back through the fabric. (This method is explained on page 24.)

Embroidered black satin drawstring bag, *circa* 1850. *Collection of Beatrice Russell*

Chrysanthemums. *Collection of the Embroiderers' Guild of NSW Inc.*

Early in the twentieth century the *Needlecraft Practical Journal on Ribbonwork* was published, giving a list of ribbons available from William Briggs & Co. Ltd, a well known purveyor of embroidery and lace supplies. Pompadour ribbon is described as being most like that used in years gone by, being about 1/8'' (3 mm) wide and available in a great variety of colours, both plain and shaded. This ribbon was ideal for working the ever popular sprays of small flowers. Giant crepe ribbon, with its slightly crinkled surface, was excellent for larger flowers such as poppies. Picotee ribbon was 5/8'' (15 mm) wide, with a fine serrated edge on one side, and was meant to be gathered at the other edge. It made perfect picotees or pinks.

At this time catalogues from Australian department stores regularly featured stamped designs and transfers for embroidery including ribbon work, or Rococo work as it was sometimes called.

Anthony Horderns' of Sydney, in their price list for Art Needlework of 1910, listed pompadour ribbon at 6 pence a dozen yards, giant crepe at 1¾d a yard or 1/8d a dozen yards, and picotee ribbon at 3½d a yard or 3/3d a dozen yards.

The embroidered frame around a coronation portrait of Queen Alexandra (*circa* 1902) combines ribbon embroidery with metal thread. The flowers and leaves are all worked in straight stitches in two shades of ribbon. Stems are in stem stitch with silk thread and the bow is Jap gold thread, couched.

The detail from a table centre (*circa* 1910) is worked on cream satin and features a basket of flowers. The raised roses are in two shades of narrow silk ribbon worked over a padding of three satin stitches in heavy cotton thread. The ribbon is worked in straight stitches overlapped. Other flowers are gathered ribbon circles and circles of tiny straight stitches. Leaves are also straight stitches. The basket and handle are outlined in chain stitch with details in running stitch. The bow is in satin stitch, using floss silk.

Top: *Needlecraft Practical Journal*, early twentieth century, and Anthony Horderns' price list of Art Needlework, June 1910

Embroidered frame, *circa* 1902, for a coronation portrait of Queen Alexandra. *Author's collection*

Detail from a tablecentre, *circa* 1910. *Collection of the Embroiderers' Guild of NSW Inc.*

All these old examples can provide inspiration for modern-day adaptations, although the ribbon embroidery being done now is much more adventurous in the use of stitches and design, and richer in the combination of materials.

Today there is a vast range of ribbons with which to work: velvet, satin, silk, polyester and rayon, all in wide to very narrow widths. Combined with stitchery in the beautiful threads available, ribbon embroidery becomes a rich and excitingly textured technique which can be applied to all sorts of things, including clothing, bags, cushions, boxes, pictures, jewellery and sewing accessories. Examples of all these articles are included in this book.

Although I prefer to encourage people to design their own work, I realise there are many who are more comfortable with a design prepared for them. I have therefore included a number of design diagrams for various items in the book. I hope that anyone using these designs will feel free to alter them, changing colours, materials or stitches. Everyone can add their own creative touch to a design. The designs can be adapted to suit many things other than the specific items illustrated.

FABRICS, RIBBONS AND EQUIPMENT

These days a vast choice of fabrics is available, many of which are suitable bases for ribbon embroidery. Firm fabrics give the best results. Velveteen and dress velvet are rich and good to work on, but avoid heavy furnishing velvets as they are too thick and difficult to pull ribbon through. If you are working on fine silk, back it with a piece of silk organza to give the fabric more body. If you wish to use velvet ribbon pulled through the fabric choose a more loosely woven fabric, in wool, cotton or linen. Otherwise, use the velvet ribbon on the surface of the fabric only.

The range of polyester, satin, nylon, silk and velvet ribbons makes ribbon embroidery very exciting. Combinations of different textures in ribbons can be most effective, using shiny satins with matt silk or nylon. There are also many fashion ribbons which come and go. If any of the ribbons that appear in this book are not available in your area, use your imagination with what is available. Sometimes this can generate an idea that leads to exciting new designs.

When buying ribbons without a specific purpose in mind two or three metres is a useful quantity. The most practical way to store ribbons is on small rolled cards. Business cards are a convenient size, with a cut in each short end to hold the ends of the ribbon. The card is rolled and held with adhesive tape. Keep each range of colour separate, either in large divided boxes or in a box for each colour. Winding ribbon around flat cards is not recommended as it makes creases in the ribbon.

The most useful threads are perle cotton Nos 5 and 8 and stranded cotton, but there are many beautiful embroidery threads that can enhance embroidery with ribbons. Silk threads and very shiny rayon threads can add a particularly good contrast. You will need sewing cotton to match the ribbons used.

Various types of needles in several sizes are essential—tapestry needles, which have a large eye and blunt point, chenille needles, also large eyed, but with sharp points, and crewel needles, which have a long eye. The finer sizes of crewel needle, 9 to 12, are the most useful.

Good embroidery scissors and a larger pair will be needed, and a stiletto or awl for piercing holes in the fabric to pull the ribbon through. An antique stiletto in steel, bone or ivory is very nice to use if you can obtain one.

An embroidery hoop can be used, but take care that the hoop does not mark the fabric, particularly if working on velvet.

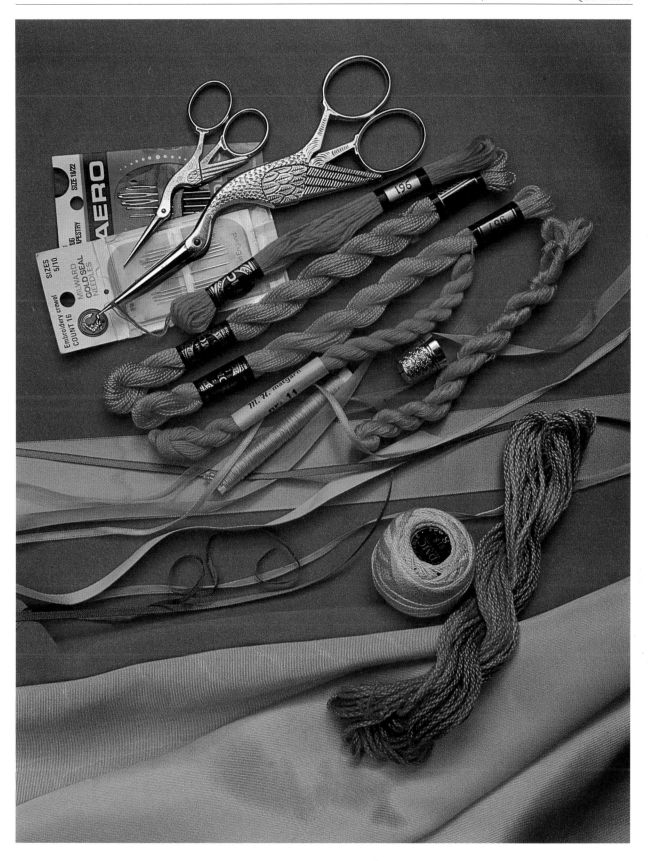

TECHNIQUES

Starting and Finishing

To start, leave about 1.5 cm of ribbon on the wrong side of the work. This is sewn down with sewing cotton when part of the work is completed. Finish in the same way. It is essential not to leave long ends behind the work as they will tangle. Some polyester ribbons are very springy and need to be sewn down at the back of the work as soon as is practical.

If it is difficult to pull a ribbon through the fabric, use a stiletto to pierce a hole for the ribbon to pass through.

When pulling the ribbon through to the back of the work check to see that the needle is not piercing a ribbon already worked, as this can make it difficult to pull through, and will distort the work.

Designing

The design must be suitable in scale for the article you are making. Always establish the size and shape of the article first, then the area to be embroidered, then the details of the design. Details of the design need only be simple, e.g. circles and ovals for flowers and leaves.

Designing for clothing needs special attention as the whole garment has to be considered as well as the person who will wear it.

Cut an extra pattern in paper and mark on it the area to be embroidered, then try it against the person who will wear it. Any adjustments can be made before working up the design of the embroidery.

If it is an important garment it is worth making a calico replica with the design marked on it. Time spent on planning and designing is time well spent and will save hours of anguished unpicking.

When working on anything with seams that will be under the embroidery, work on each piece of the article to within about 3 cm of the seam, sew up the seam, press on the wrong side then complete the embroidery over the seam

Transferring Designs

Only a very simple outline of the design needs to be transferred to the fabric to be embroidered.

For small pieces such as brooches or needle cases you need only mark the placement of the largest elements of the design with a dot in pencil or water soluble fabric marking pen. The rest of the design can be followed from the drawing.

For larger or more specific designs, outline the design on paper with a black felt pen so that it is very clear. Tape this to a flat surface with adhesive tape. Lay a piece of nylon net over the design and attach it with adhesive tape. Go over the outline of the design with a black marking pen, then remove the net and place in position on the fabric to be embroidered. Pin or baste securely in place. Now go over the outline on the net with a water soluble fabric marking pen. When you remove the net, the outline of the design will appear on the fabric as a series of dots. These dots can be removed when the embroidery is finished by holding a cotton bud dampened with water against them.

When transferring a design from a book by this method, place a piece of firm clear plastic over the design before tracing it with a felt pen.

Finishing

Your finished ribbon embroidery can be pressed lightly, on the wrong side, into a well padded surface—a folded towel is ideal. Take care not to flatten the embroidery.

When mounting pictures, make sure the mount is perfectly squared at the corners. If possible, use acid free board.

When working with glue, work over clean scrap paper and change the paper at every stage of the construction.

A large darning needle is ideal for spreading glue and for applying a small spot of glue to a small area.

STITCHES AND FLOWERS

When working with ribbon, you will have to make the stitches large enough for the scale of the ribbon and work rather more loosely than is usual with thread.

Make sure the needle is large enough to take the ribbon comfortably.

If you want the ribbon flat, hold it in place with your thumb while pulling it through the fabric. It can sometimes be effective to let the ribbon twist.

Use stitches that have most of the stitch on the right side of the work—herringbone, chain and Cretan stitches all have a minimum of the stitch on the reverse side.

Stitches threaded with ribbons can make rich patterns. Use a firm thread such as perle cotton for the groundwork stitch. A great many effects can be achieved with straight stitches, particularly when working flowers, as you will see from the illustrations in the book.

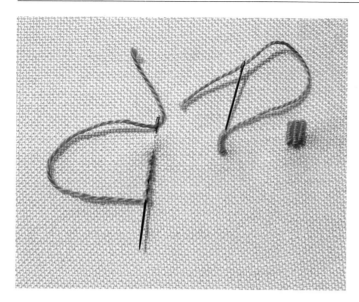

Bullion knot

A most useful stitch for centres of flowers, wheat ears, small leaves, etc.
1. Make a stitch as shown, bringing the eye of the needle almost through the fabric.
2. Wind the thread around several times, depending how long the stitch is to be.
3. Pull the needle and thread through the twists, holding the twists firmly in one hand.
4. Take the needle down as shown to complete the stitch.

Buttonhole stitch

Bring the needle and thread out on the line of the lower edge of the stitch. Make a stitch as shown, with the thread looped under the needle.

At the right of the picture, two rows of buttonhole stitch are shown worked brick fashion.

This is a very versatile stitch and can be worked well spaced, as shown, closely or unevenly. A circle of closely worked buttonhole stitch makes a round flower.

Chain stitch (picture on lower left)

Bring the needle and thread or ribbon through from the back, put the needle in again beside this, and bring it out underneath, with the thread under the needle. Continue in the same way.

When working with ribbon, keep the ribbon flat and do not pull the stitch up tightly.

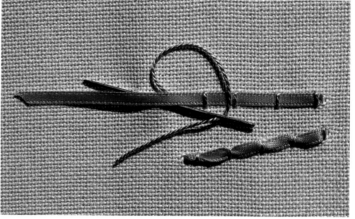

Couching

Lay a piece of ribbon along the line to be covered, and with another thread, tie it down with a small stitch at intervals.

Cretan stitch

Note that the needle always points inwards, with the thread under it. Cretan stitch is very versatile as it can be worked closely or spaced evenly or unevenly, so that many different textures can be created with it.

Cross stitch

This can be worked as a straight or diagonal cross. A cross in the opposite direction can be worked over the centre in a finer thread. In clusters, cross stitch makes an attractive group of small flowers.

Detached chain stitch

This stitch can be worked with a short or long stitch at the end.

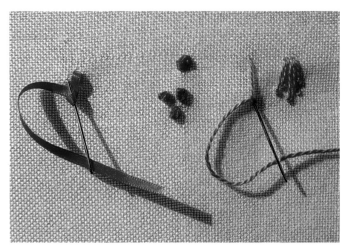

French knot

1. Bring the thread or ribbon through to the front of the work, twist it once only around the needle, pull snugly around the needle, then insert the needle into the fabric close to the starting point and pull through to the back.

2. Hold the thread firmly with the thumb while pulling through. When working with satin ribbon leave the knot slightly looser than normal while pulling the ribbon through to the back.

A long-tailed French knot is shown at the right in the illustration. For this, after twisting the thread round the needle take it down to the length required and finish the stitch in the usual way.

Fly stitch

This is a most versatile stitch and can be worked singly, in groups, with long or short tails, in horizontal or vertical rows. It is very good for ferns or feathery foliage.

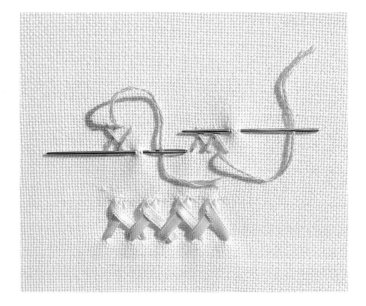

Herringbone stitch

This stitch can be worked very close or well spaced. It is ideal for working over ribbon on a curved line. It also looks very effective worked in perle cotton and threaded with ribbon.

Ladder stitch

This is a very good method for stitching two pieces together on the right side.

Pick up the fold on the seam line with the needle, bring the needle and thread through and pick up the fold of the other piece. Continue in this way, making the stitches at right angles to the folds and drawing them up so that the two folded edges are joined invisibly.

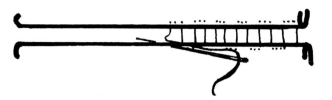

Raised stem band

1. First work a 'ladder' of straight stitches.
2. Then work stem stitch over these bars, not going through the fabric. Work rows side by side, placing them closely until the whole ladder is filled.
3. The rows may be worked all in the same direction or up and down.

For a rounded effect, work a padding of straight stitches in wool yarn under the bars before working the stem stitch.

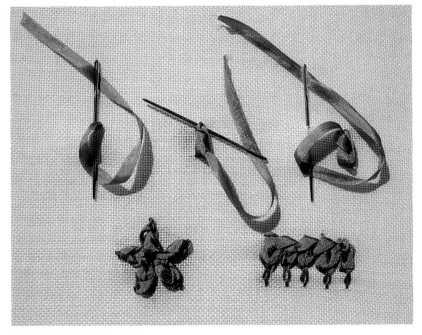

Rosette chain stitch

This stitch is worked from right to left.
1. Work a twisted chain stitch.
2. Pass the needle under the top of the stitch, taking care not to pull it up tightly.

This is a rather loose stitch and really needs another small stitch at the end to hold it down. Two ways of using it are illustrated—the row of stitches has a small chain stitch on the end, and the flower is finished with a French knot.

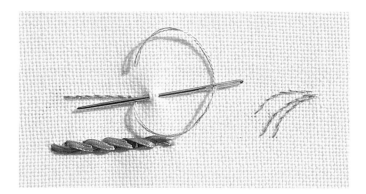

Stem stitch

This can be worked as a fine line or in rows to form a filling.

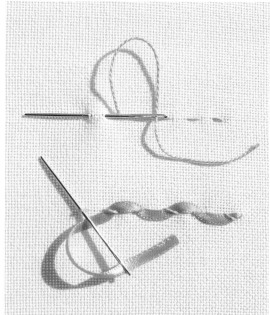

Threaded running stitch

Work a row of running stitch, then thread in and out of the running stitch with a ribbon or thread.

Twisted chain stitch

The needle goes into the fabric over the thread before making the chain. In ribbon this stitch makes a good bud.

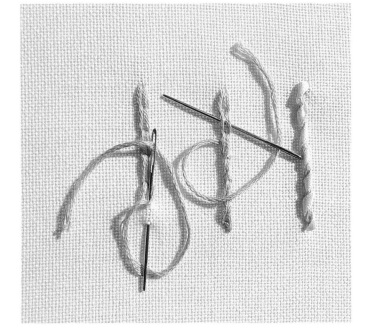

Whipped chain stitch

Work a row of continuous chain stitch then whip over each stitch with the same thread or a contrasting colour.

Ruched ribbon

Running stitch is worked in zig-zag along the ribbon and then drawn up.

The resulting flexible braid can be used in a number of ways. Examples can be found throughout the book.

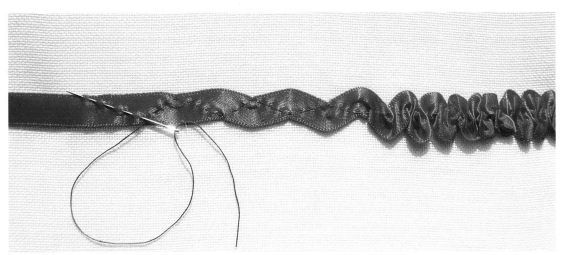

Sewing on beads

Bring the needle out where the bead is to be sewn, thread the bead, position it on the fabric and take the needle down close to the bead and under it, coming up where the next bead is required. If sewing on a single bead in an isolated position, sew through the bead twice before fastening off.

Carnation

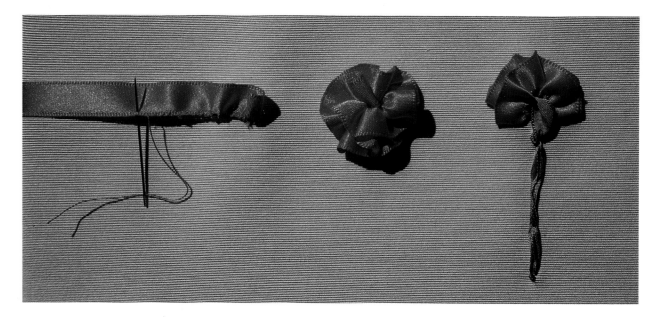

1. Using sewing cotton whip over one edge of the ribbon with fairly small stitches and gather up.
2. For a full flower sew one end of the gathered ribbon to the fabric, in the centre of the flower, then coil the gathered ribbon around this until the flower is full enough. Sew down as invisibly as possible.

3. For a flower in profile work two rows of gathered ribbon, starting with the top row. It is best to work two separate rows, one over the other. Turn in the raw edges and sew neatly to the fabric, sewing the row into place as well.

Chrysanthemum

It is best to use soft ribbon for this flower. A stiff ribbon does not hold the twist well. For learning the technique, the nylon strip sold for knitting and crochet is excellent.

Small delicate flowers can be worked in silk ribbon.
1. Using a short length of ribbon, about 15 cm, bring the ribbon through the fabric and twist in a clockwise direction—Figure 1 (see next page).
2. Hold the twisted ribbon down with one thumb at the length required for the petal, make a loose loop with the other hand and slip it under the thumb—Figure 2.
3. Put the needle into the fabric in the centre of the loop and pull through to the back until you have a neat curl—Figure 3.

Note: Twisting the ribbon in a clockwise direction will give a curl to the right. If a left-hand curl is required twist anticlockwise.

Leave the twisted ribbon fairly loose above where it is held down to give a nice curve to the petal.

The curls need to be sewn down; one or two stitches in sewing cotton will be enough.

Each petal should be cut off at the back of the work and the end sewn down. This can be done after working several petals.

To achieve a well shaped flower, mark an oval of dots in pencil the size required. Mark the centre of the flower with a dot.

Centres can be worked in loose straight stitches, loops of ribbon or French knots. The addition of some small beads gives an extra sparkle.

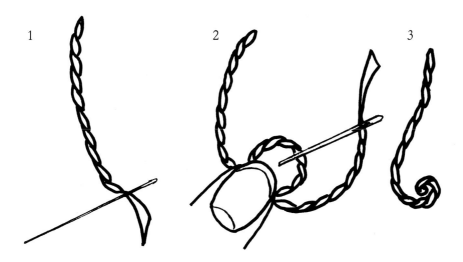

Folded rose

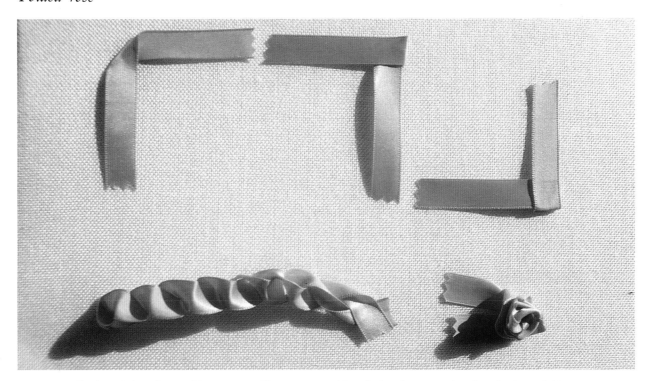

Have a needle threaded with matching cotton. Use 1.5 cm ribbon or wider until you are familiar with the method. If you have a long length of ribbon, do not cut it.

1. Make a fold about 25 cm from one end, as illustrated in the top left of the photograph.
2. Fold right side over the left (top centre).
3. Fold lower end up (top right).
4. Repeat 2 and 3 until you come to the end of the short length of ribbon. There should be about twenty folds.

5. Hold ends firmly in one hand and release folds (bottom left) and then pull the longer end of ribbon with the other hand, slowly until the rose forms (bottom right).
6. Stitch the rose through the centre once or twice, and through the petals, as invisibly as possible. This will secure it.
7. Cut the ends, fold back neatly and sew onto the fabric.

Spider's web rose

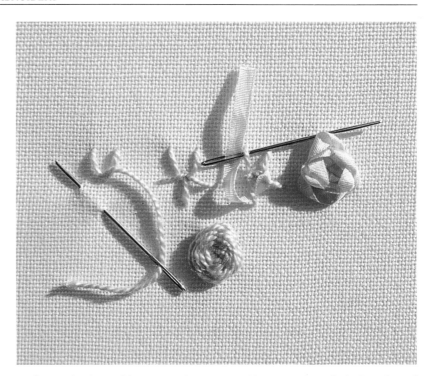

1. Using a firm thread work a fly stitch, then add a straight stitch each side of the fly stitch into a central point.
2. Bring the thread or ribbon through at the centre and weave it over and under the spokes until the web is filled.

When using ribbon, weave it fairly loosely and let it twist occasionally—the result is a rose-like circle.

Pin roses

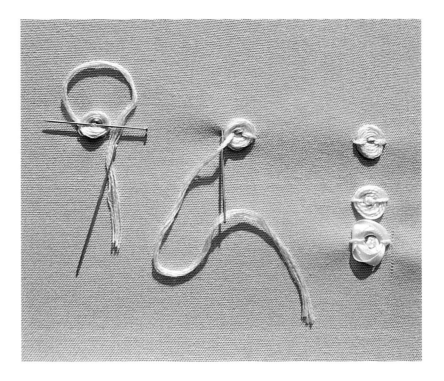

Put a pin through the fabric where the rose is to be worked, taking up as little of the fabric as possible. Bring the thread through at this point and wind it around the pin several times until the required size is achieved. Take the thread to the back just underneath the last coil. Make a small stitch over all the coils, at each side.

The example shows a pin rose being worked with six strands of stranded cotton. There are also examples worked in perle cotton No. 8 and 3 mm silk ribbon. These have a French knot worked at the centre.

Rolled rosebud

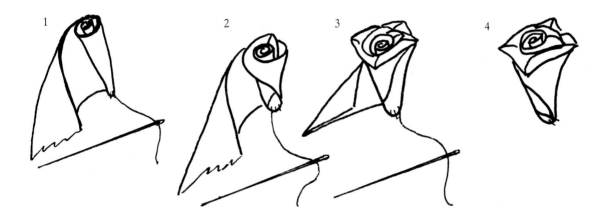

Have a needle threaded with matching cotton.

1. Make a tight roll on one end of the ribbon, stitch at one side—Figure 1.
2. Fold the ribbon as illustrated and turn around the centre roll. Keep the ribbon out and towards the top of the roll, not tightly against the roll, and stitch again—Figure 2.

3. Fold again and turn, stitching at the base—Figure 3.
4. Cut the ribbon straight across and fold over to make a point. Take this around the rose and stitch firmly—Figure 4.

These roses will sit flat on the fabric, not standing up. They look well in a small group or among other flowers.

Wound rose

1. Make a loose knot in one end of the ribbon 1 cm from the end. Sew this end to the fabric where the centre of the flower is to be.
2. Fold the knot over and pin to the fabric with a long needle.
3. Wind the ribbon around the needle, twisting the ribbon occasionally, until there is enough for a full rose. Do not pull the ribbon tightly around the needle, but keep it fairly loose, especially at the centre turns.

4. With sewing cotton, stitch the ribbon as invisibly as possible in strategic places so that it will hold together.
5. Remove the needle and if necessary add more stitching. Some ribbons are rather stiff and do not wind around the needle easily; they may need to be stitched as you wind.

This rose is pictured over the page.

Wound rose (page 27)

Gathered rose

You will need
15 cm of 4 mm silk ribbon in a deep pink
15 cm of 4 mm silk ribbon in a medium pink
25 cm of 4 mm silk ribbon in a light pink
sewing cotton to match the ribbons

1. Gather about 8 cm of the deepest pink ribbon, whipping over the edge of the ribbon (see carnation illustration). Do not cut the ribbon until it is gathered.

Try to keep the gathered ribbon from spiralling by holding the starting end in the first and second fingers of the left hand while gathering. Finish off and cut off surplus ribbon.

Pin the gathered ribbon in place—first slide the pins through the ribbon and fabric once only, in a tight oval as illustrated. Sew in place as invisibly as possible.

2. Gather about 10 cm of the medium pink ribbon, cut off surplus, then pin and sew in place around the first gathered oval. It is important to make a good shape with this piece of ribbon, as the finished rose depends on it.

3. With the light pink ribbon make large stitches, left a little loose, around the gathered ribbons to suggest the outer petals of the rose. This is really a large stem stitch.

It is best to work this rose in a frame or embroidery hoop.

Wild rose

You will need to frame the fabric in an embroidery hoop to work this flower. Take a 30 cm length of 7 mm silk ribbon and thread it into a tapestry or chenille needle.
1. Bring six loops of ribbon through the fabric, in a circle, taking care to keep the ribbon flat and making the loops the same length.

2. With two strands of stranded cotton in a matching colour work three straight stitches at the base of each petal, laying one straight stitch at the centre with a shorter stitch each side.
3. Fill the centre with French knots in three strands of stranded cotton or perle cotton No. 8.

This rose can also be worked in 7 mm polyester satin ribbon, as shown in the illustration.

Rosebuds

1. Thread two shades of 4 mm silk ribbon into a tapestry needle and make two straight stitches, almost on top of one another.
2. With two strands of stranded cotton in a green to tone with the rosebud make three pairs of straight stitches around the bud. Start with the central stitches, and make each pair not quite the same length. Stalks can be added in stem stitch.

Examples of this rosebud appear in the Basket of Flowers on page 100 and the Floral Spray box top on page 124.

Lavender

1. Using 4 mm silk ribbon, make a straight stitch at the top of the flower head. Then make alternate slanting stitches each side of the first stitch, and continue until the required size is reached.
2. Stalks can be in twisted silk ribbon, as shown in the illustration, making a long straight stitch for the stalk. This must be sewn down as invisibly as possible, into the twists of the ribbon. Stem

stitch is another alternative for the stem, or whipped chain stitch.

The Basket of flowers on page 100 includes lavender sprays.

Iris

1. Take 20 cm lengths of both 7 mm silk ribbon and 7 mm organza ribbon and thread them into the one tapestry needle. Work three straight stitches with the two ribbons to form the lower petals of the iris. Always work from the outside into the central point of the flower.

2. With 7 mm silk ribbon in the same colour or a shade deeper, and a contrast colour in 7 mm organza ribbon, both in the needle, make three small stitches of uneven length, working from the outside into the centre, to form the upper petals. Leave the stitches fairly loose so that the petals curve nicely. It may be necessary to put a stitch in sewing cotton to hold the petals in the desired shape.

3. Stalks can be twisted ribbon, as in the illustration, or whipped chain. The iris needs a firm stem, not too thin.

The iris is used in the Basket of Flowers on page 100

Periwinkle

1. First work a curved trail in stem stitch, using two strands of stranded cotton in green.

2. With the same thread work small detached chains each side of the stem stitch, varying the direction of the stitches a little. This gives a less rigid effect.

3. With 7 mm silk ribbon pull small loops through the fabric where the flowers are required. Make a small French knot in the centre of each loop, using two strands of stranded cotton in a darker shade than the ribbon. Draw the knot down firmly. The loops must be sewn down on the back of the work so that they do not work through to the front.

4. For buds or profile flowers make small loops and anchor them with a small stitch on the underside of the loop.

The periwinkle can be seen in the Basket of Flowers on page 100.

Fuchsia

1. Using soft ribbon bring three loops through the fabric as illustrated.
2. Stitch through each loop with a small stitch. Do not pull the loop tightly.
3. With satin ribbon wider than the soft ribbon, work four straight stitches as shown. Always come through the fabric outside the flower and make each stitch with a twist, leaving it rather loose.

4. Stitch these petals with sewing cotton as invisibly as possible.
5. Add stamens in two strands of stranded cotton, using a long-tailed French knot.

The stamens must appear to come from a central point at the base of the flower.

BEGINNERS' PROJECTS

Needlecase Set

This charming set consists of a needlecase, scissors case and pinwheel. The set illustrated has been made in a furnishing moiré, but linen, heavy silk, rayon or velveteen would all be suitable. The best results will be obtained by using tones of similar colours, with a small amount of a contrasting colour.

Use the design given here, or work out a simple design of your own.

You will need
30 cm fabric
interfacing 26 × 13.5 cm
flannel 26 × 13.5 cm
2 m of 3 mm satin ribbon to tone with the fabric
1.5 m of 3 mm satin ribbon in another tone
2 m each of two tones of 3 mm silk or soft polyester ribbon
1 m of 5 mm satin ribbon with a picot edge, to tone with the fabric
stranded cotton in a tone of the main colour and a contrasting colour
sewing cotton to match the fabric
firm, thin card or plastic 12 × 16 cm approx. (plastic from an icecream container is ideal)

Needlecase

1. Cut a piece of fabric 30 × 17 cm. This allows for 1.5 cm turnings all round. On one 17 cm end mark a curved line. Use a sharp pencil or water soluble fabric marking pen, and make dots rather than a continuous line.
2. Mark the centres of the larger circles of the design on the fabric 2 cm in from the curved line.
3. Work spider's webs over these dots in the silk or polyester ribbon. Start in the centre of the curve and work outwards, graduating the webs to the outer edge.
4. Now work the large French knots and loops in satin ribbon. Make sure you sew the loops securely on the wrong side.
5. The small crosses are worked next, with four small stitches into a central point.

6. Work fly stitch in groups of two and three stitches around the edge of the design, using two strands of stranded cotton, with French knots in the same thread at the ends of the fly stitches.
7. Small French knots in a contrasting colour, worked in two strands of stranded cotton, complete the embroidery.

To make up
1. Cut a piece of interfacing 26 × 13.5 cm, and cut a curve at one end, the same as the curve on the fabric.
2. Lightly press the embroidery on the wrong side, into a well-padded surface.
3. Fold the embroidery over the interfacing and baste into place, folding the corners neatly. To get a good curved edge, gather the fabric slightly, using a running stitch, until it curves over the interfacing. See picture on page 34.
4. Press lightly.
5. Cut the flannel to fit the prepared needlecase so that the edge of the flannel is about 0.5 cm within the edge. Baste into place carefully, so that the stitches do not come through to the right side of the work. Pin the picot-edged ribbon over the basted edge of the flannel and sew down through the picots, again taking care not to stitch through to the right side of the needlecase.
6. Fold the straight edge up for 6 cm and sew up the sides with neat, small stitches in sewing cotton to match the fabric. This forms the pocket to hold the scissors case and pinwheel.

Pinwheel

1. Cut two circles of card or plastic 5 cm in diameter.
2. Work a small circular spray in the same ribbons and threads as for the needlecase on a piece of fabric.
3. Cut the embroidered fabric and one other piece into circles 1.5 cm larger than the card or plastic.
4. Taking care to centre the embroidery, gather the fabric tightly over each circle of card or plastic.
5. Sew the two covered circles together with small neat stitches.

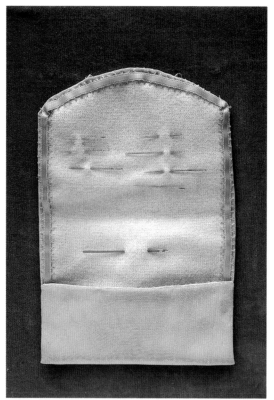

The needlecase opened out

Key

 French knots

 straight stitches

 loops

 fly stitches

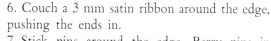 spider's webs

6. Couch a 3 mm satin ribbon around the edge, pushing the ends in.

7. Stick pins around the edge. Berry pins in addition to ordinary pins look very decorative.

Scissors Case

1. In card or thin plastic cut two shapes to fit your scissors.

2. Work a small design in the same ribbons and threads used on the needlecase. Cut out the embroidered fabric and three other pieces 1 cm larger than the card or plastic shape. Fold the embroidered fabric and one of the other pieces over the two card or plastic shapes and glue carefully.

3. Line the covered shapes with the other pieces of fabric, turning the edges under and sewing them neatly to the covered pieces.

4. Sew the two covered and lined pieces together, leaving an opening at the top large enough for the scissors to be inserted. The bows of the scissors should protrude a little.

5. Couch matching 3 mm ribbon around the curved edge of the case, starting with the top of the back piece. The ends of the ribbon can be pushed inside the case. Then, starting at the bottom of the case, couch ribbon around the edge, finishing off with a turned-under edge.

Embroidery design for needlecase set

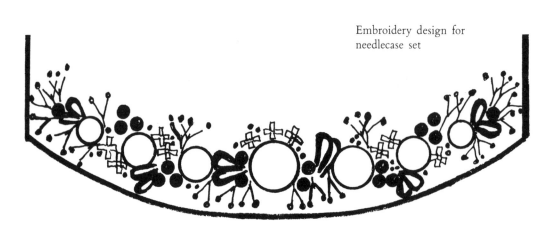

Two Needlecases

These needlecases are each made from 25 cm of 7.5 cm wide ribbon. A piece of fabric 25 × 10 cm could be substituted.

The blue flowers are made by bringing loops 2 cm long of 7 mm ribbon through the fabric; the ends of the loops are turned under to form a point and stitched down. The loops are close together and there are three to each flower. French knots form the centre and there is a line of Cretan stitch in one strand of stranded cotton circling the flowers. Groups of Cretan stitch in a deeper shade are worked over the first row.

French knots in a contrast colour are added at the ends of some of the Cretan stitches.

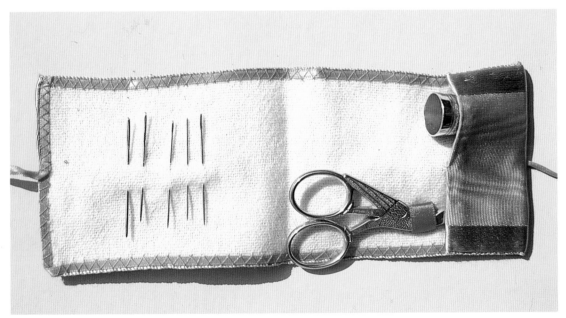

One of the needlecases opened out

Blue Flowers

Floral Spray

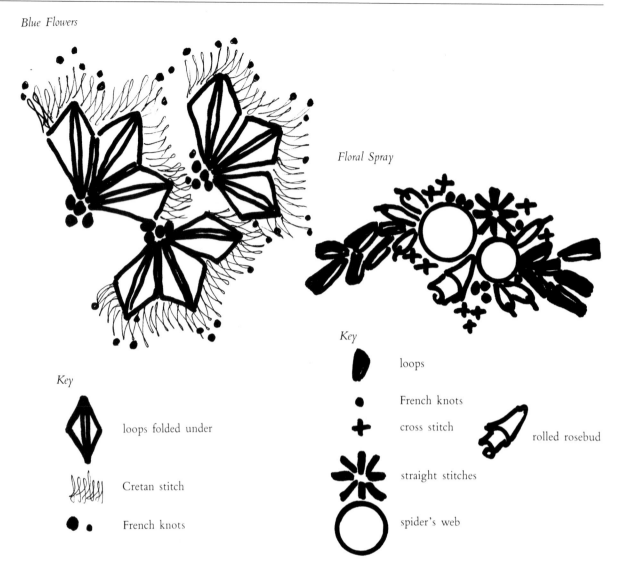

Key

loops folded under

Cretan stitch

French knots

Key

loops

French knots

cross stitch

straight stitches

spider's web

rolled rosebud

The pink floral spray on the second needlecase consists of spider's webs in old shaded ribbon, unfortunately no longer obtainable. Two shades of ribbon could be substituted.

There is a rolled rosebud in satin ribbon, and a daisy in straight stitches in satin ribbon. Groups of French knots and cross stitches in satin ribbon lie around the flowers, and groups of loops form leaves at each end of the spray.

The needlecases are made up in similar fashion to the needlecase on page 32, lined with flannel and hemmed up and stitched at one end to hold scissors and a thimble.

A length of ribbon is sewn to each end and tied in a bow to close the needlecase.

Flower Sampler

This sampler is illustrated on page 17.

Daisy
1. Use 3 mm silk or polyester ribbon, green and yellow perle cotton No. 8.
2. Two straight stitches are used for each petal. Work the flower centres with a French knot.
3. Work the leaves in fly stitch.

Heath
1. Use 3 mm pink satin ribbon, 3 mm green silk ribbon, green stranded cotton, white perle cotton No. 8.
2. Work the flowers in straight stitches in pink satin ribbon, with a fly stitch with a long tail over the straight stitch using white perle cotton.
3. Work the leaves in fly stitch in silk ribbon and stranded cotton.

Forget-me-not
1. Use 3 mm blue silk or polyester ribbon, yellow perle cotton No. 8, green stranded cotton.
2. Work the flowers in five small straight stitches with a French knot in the centre in perle cotton.
3. Work the stalks in fly stitch and the leaves in detached chain stitch, using four strands of stranded cotton.

Fuchsia
1. Use 5 mm magenta satin ribbon, 3 mm purple silk or polyester ribbon, 3 mm green silk or polyester ribbon, sewing cotton to match the purple ribbon, green stranded cotton.
2. The flower is three loops of purple ribbon sewn down at the tips.
3. Add four straight stitches, twisted, in magenta satin ribbon.
4. The half-open flower is all straight stitches, as are the bud and leaves.
5. The stems are worked in stem stitch.

Violet
1. Use 3 mm silk or polyester ribbon, green stranded cotton.
2. The flowers are worked in straight stitches, two to each petal.
3. The leaves are worked in stem stitch.

Wattle
1. Use 3 mm yellow silk or polyester ribbon in yellow and green, yellow perle cotton No. 8, green stranded cotton.
2. Work leaves first in straight stitches in ribbon, two stitches to each leaf.
3. Work flowers in silk ribbon in French knots, with knots in perle cotton at the tips of the sprays.
4. Work the stem in stem stitch using stranded cotton.

Waratah
1. Use 3 mm silk or polyester ribbon in two shades of red, 5 mm dark red satin ribbon, red perle cotton No. 5, green stranded cotton.
2. Work straight stitches in two shades of red ribbon.
3. Work the French knots at the top of the flower in perle cotton.
4. The sepals are worked in straight stitches, twisted, in dark red satin ribbon.
5. Work the leaves in fly stitch, using three strands of stranded cotton.

Flannel flower
1. Use 3 mm white silk or polyester ribbon, green stranded cotton.
2. Work the flowers in detached twisted chain stitches.
3. Satin-stitch the centre in stranded cotton.
4. Work the leaves in fly stitch using four strands of stranded cotton.

Wisteria
1. Use 3 mm mauve silk or polyester ribbon, green stranded cotton.
2. Work the flowers in detached chain stitch with small straight stitches at the tips of the sprays.
3. Work the stalks in stem stitch in three strands of stranded cotton.

Pinks
1. Use 5 mm pink satin ribbon, 3 mm green silk ribbon, pink sewing cotton.
2. Gather one edge of the pink satin ribbon and sew it into a circle for the full flowers.
3. Make profile flowers out of two lengths of gathered ribbon, sewn down one under the other.
4. Work the stems in stem stitch and leaves in straight stitches, both in green silk ribbon.

DESIGNS FOR CLOTHING

Carnation Spray

This design was originally worked on the very full sleeves of an evening blouse of wool crepe. It would be equally suitable embroidered on a skirt, pocket, jacket or jumper. The quantities quoted are for one motif only.

You will need

1 m each of 10 mm velvet ribbon and 10 mm satin ribbon in the same colour, and sewing thread to match

1 m each of 20 mm gauze ribbon and 35 mm shaded gauze ribbon, in similar colours (satin or nylon ribbon may be substituted)

1 m of 1.5 mm satin ribbon in another colour

1 m narrow gold braid or satin ribbon, and sewing cotton to match

2 m silk or soft polyester ribbon in a colour to tone with the wider ribbons

stranded cotton in a darker shade of the 1.5 mm satin ribbon and in a lighter shade of the background colour

beads in a light bright colour to tone with the wider ribbons

Method

1. Following the diagram on page 40, mark on the fabric, with either a water soluble pen or basting thread, the centres of the carnations, the lines of the sprays of flowers and the stems.

2. With 20 mm ribbon make one full carnation profile flower and a bud (see page 24 for instructions).

3. Fold the 35 mm ribbon almost in half and make one full carnation, a profile flower and a bud.

4. Sew these flowers in place as invisibly as possible, adding twisted chain stitches in silk ribbon at the base of the profile flowers and buds.

5. Sew the gold braid or ribbon along the stem lines with matching sewing cotton.

6. Work the larger sprays of flowers in 1.5 mm satin ribbon with five single chains in a circle for each flower. Work another chain in six strands of stranded cotton inside the ribbon chains. The buds at the ends of the sprays are single chains in ribbon with chains in stranded cotton outside them.

7. Work stems to these sprays in whipped chain stitch, using four strands of stranded cotton.

8. Sew a bead in the centre of each flower.

9. Using one strand of cotton work the beaded sprays. Start at the top of the spray and sew three or four beads close together, *make a straight stitch directly underneath them. Take the needle out to the left about 3 mm and sew on three beads, then make a straight stitch from the beads to the centre. Repeat to the right, then repeat from * until the spray is completed.

10. Work stems in one strand of cotton in stem stitch.

11. Stitch the satin ribbon to the back of the velvet ribbon with a small zig-zag stitch on the sewing machine, sewing along each edge.

12. Cut 0.5 m of this prepared ribbon and tie a bow in the centre. Fold the two ends under the knot to form a double bow, and sew to the centre of the knot.

13. Fold the rest of the ribbon in half and sew the fold to the back of bow at the knot.

14. Pin the bow in place over the stems of the design, pin out the ribbon similarly to the illustration, and sew down with matching thread.

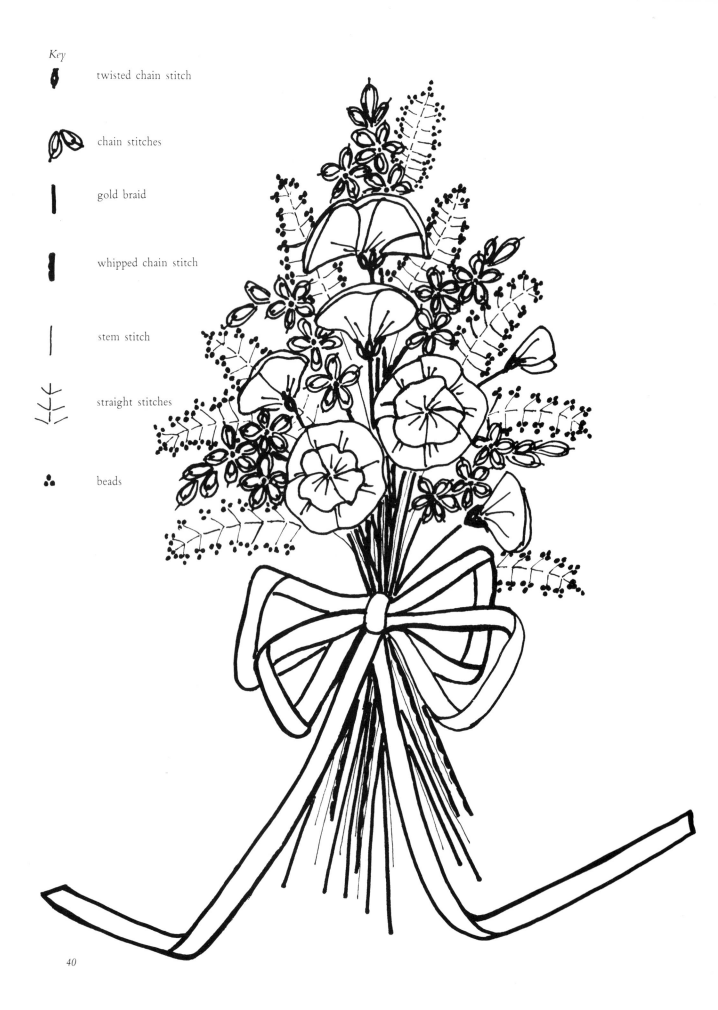

Key

	twisted chain stitch
	chain stitches
	gold braid
	whipped chain stitch
	stem stitch
	straight stitches
	beads

Rose Chain

This pretty chain of roses can be embroidered on knitwear, blouses, dresses or children's wear, and looks well in many different colour combinations.

The illustration is worked on a commercially made knitted wool vest and the quantities quoted are for this garment.

You will need
6 m silk or soft polyester 3 mm ribbon in the main colour
4 m silk or soft polyester 3 mm ribbon in another tone
4 m of 1.5 mm satin ribbon in a contrasting colour
4 m silk or soft polyester 3 mm ribbon in another colour
stranded cotton in the main colour, in another shade of this colour, and in the contrasting . colour

Method
1. Starting with the large central rose, work a spider's web in silk or polyester ribbon in the main colour.
2. On each side of the rose work three French knots in contrasting satin ribbon.
3. On each side of the knots work a smaller spider's web in the other tone of the main colour in silk or polyester ribbon, followed by three more knots in satin ribbon and one underneath the rose, then a twisted chain and a small spider's web in silk or polyester ribbon in the main colour.
4. In a contrasting colour of silk or polyester ribbon work groups of fly stitches under the roses.
5. Work fly stitches in two strands of stranded cotton over the ribbon stitches, using a similar colour.
6. Groups of three Cretan stitches in two strands

Key

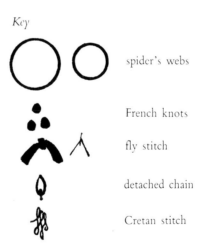

spider's webs

French knots

fly stitch

detached chain

Cretan stitch

of stranded cotton in the main colour, are worked each side of the fly stitches under the largest rose, and also above it, and each side of the twisted chain stitch.

7. Small detached chains, in two strands of stranded cotton in a tone of the main colour, are worked above some of the roses.

8. The pattern is repeated as often as required.

You may have to adjust the pattern to fit the article you are embroidering, as at the point of the V of the vest illustrated. This is not difficult and usually means condensing the pattern slightly. When embroidering a design on something like the vest, start at the centre front—the V in this case—and work each side alternately to get an even balance.

Key

loops of velvet ribbon

French knots

fly stitch

detached chain

Falling Petals

This design could fill an area such as a yoke on a jacket or dress, or a shape on a cushion. It could also be adapted to make an all-over pattern for a bag, or for a band of embroidery on clothing, on sleeves for instance.

As the velvet ribbon is pulled through the fabric, a more loosely woven fabric than usual is advisable. The illustration is worked on a wool flannel, but coarse linen or cotton would also be suitable.

The use of a stiletto to make holes for the velvet ribbon to pass through is recommended.

The design looks best in soft tones of two close colours, such as the greys and creams in the illustration.

The illustration is of a section 16 × 10 cm, and the quantities quoted are for this size.

Multiply these quantities for the number of repeats you need.

You will need
fabric for the item to be made
2 m each of 10 mm and 14 mm velvet ribbon in
    two shades of the same colour
3 m of 3 mm satin ribbon in another colour
broder cotton to match the velvet ribbons
synthetic raffia in a similar tone
perle cotton No. 5 and a shiny embroidery thread
    to match the velvet ribbons
sewing cotton to match the velvet ribbons

Method
1. Start with the large petals, which are loops of velvet ribbon pulled through the fabric, the ends turned under and stitched down to make a point.
2. Work clusters of French knots in synthetic raffia at the centre of each group of velvet petals.
3. Fly stitch in satin ribbon is worked under the velvet petals, followed by the same stitch in broder cotton.
4. Work long detached chains in shiny thread, followed by small French knots in perle cotton No. 5, to fill in the area.

Trellis

This design is suitable as a border for a jacket or yoke, or for a cushion.

The illustration is worked on wool flannel but linen, velvet, velveteen, firm cotton or polyester would be equally suitable.

The quantities quoted are for a design section 20 cm long. Multiply these quantities by the number of repeats you require.

The design looks best in a close range of colours.

You will need
fabric for the item you are making
25 cm each of 10 mm velvet ribbon, 5 mm velvet
   ribbon and 8 mm soft nylon or polyester ribbon
2 m of 3 mm satin ribbon
2 m of 1.5 mm satin ribbon
perle cotton No. 5
a shiny rayon or silk embroidery thread
stranded cotton in the same colour
monofilament nylon thread

Method
1. First arrange the trellis, laying the two velvet ribbons side by side about 1.5 cm apart and pinning them to the fabric.
2. Weave the soft 8 mm ribbon over and under the velvet ribbons, and pin.
3. Sew the ribbons down with monofilament nylon thread so that the stitches show as little as possible.
4. Work groups of French knots in 1.5 mm satin ribbon and perle cotton No. 5, as shown in the diagram.
5. Then work loops of 3 mm satin ribbon.
6. Small detached chain stitches are added next, in shiny thread, and then sprays of stem stitch in shiny thread and one strand of stranded cotton.

Key

——————————— velvet and nylon ribbons

● ●   French knots

loops

detached chains

stem stitch

Fuchsia Trail

This design was worked each side of the yoke of a dressing gown. Because the knit velour fabric of the garment is very difficult to pull ribbon through, the embroidery was worked on a wide velvet ribbon, then applied to the yoke of the gown.

The design would also look well on a blouse or jumper, perhaps on one side only.

Quantities are quoted for one trail only, approximately 28 cm long.

You will need
1 m each of two shades of 4 mm satin ribbon
2 m of 3 mm silk or soft polyester ribbon in a
    contrasting colour
1 m each of two other shades of silk or soft
    polyester ribbon
1 m of 1.5 mm satin ribbon in another colour
stranded cotton in a dark shade to tone with the
    garment
perle cotton No. 8 in a lighter shade to tone with
    the garment
stranded cotton in a lighter shade to tone with
    the 4 mm ribbon
1 m of 5 cm velvet ribbon, if working on this is
    preferred

Method
1. Transfer the curving line of the design to the cut-out yoke of the garment or the wide velvet ribbon with either a water soluble fabric marking pen or basting.
2. Mark with a dot the placement of the flowers and buds.
3. Using six strands of stranded cotton work the curving line in stem stitch.
4. Work fuchsias in the silk or polyester ribbons and satin ribbons (see instructions on page 31).
5. Work half open flowers, making three straight stitches close together in silk or polyester ribbon with three stitches over them in 1.5 mm satin ribbon, and a small straight stitch at the top of the flowers.
6. Work buds in silk or polyester ribbon, making two straight stitches almost on top of one another and a very small straight stitch at the top.
7. Work groups of leaves in perle cotton No. 8 in single chains.

If the design is worked on wide ribbon, it can be applied to the yoke with a machine stitch as illustrated or handsewn. If hand sewing, sew down with a stem stitch in matching thread on both edges.

Key

stem stitch

chain stitches

long-tailed
French knots

Butterflies and Flowers

The butterflies in this design have been made on the sewing machine, and the flowers are hand embroidered.

This is a rather free design that could be interpreted in a number of ways and adapted to suit individual requirements. The method of working the butterflies and the flower spikes is described and illustrated, but the assembling of these elements to form a design is up to you.

The illustration has been worked on polyester jersey across the shoulder and neckline of a short-sleeved top.

Butterflies

You will need
satin 23 cm square (for 3 or 4 butterflies)
cotton 23 cm square in a toning colour
23 cm square fusible web
shaded machine embroidery cotton to tone with
   the satin
crystal beads (5 for each butterfly)

Method
1. Bond the satin and cotton together with the fusible web, carefully following the instructions with the latter.
2. Transfer the design of the butterflies to the bonded fabric, having the centre of each butterfly on the straight grain of the fabric.
3. Using the shaded machine embroidery cotton, satin stitch by machine around the outlines of the butterflies.
4. Cut out the butterflies as close as possible to the satin stitch, taking care not to cut the stitching. If this does happen, place the butterfly in a piece of typing paper and satin stitch over the edge again, then tear the paper away.
5. Sew the butterflies in place on the embroidery by hand, using the machine embroidery cotton and sewing in strategic places over the satin stitch.
6. Sew the crystal beads down the bodies of the butterflies through the background fabric.

Flowers

You will need
3 mm silk or soft polyester ribbon in three
    colours—5 m of each would be enough for a
    top similar to the one illustrated
stranded cotton for stems
stranded cotton in lighter or darker shades of the
    colours of the ribbons
small round beads for flower centres

Method
1. Work each flower with six single rosette chain
stitches in silk or polyester ribbon. Over these
stitches work a single chain stitch in one strand
of stranded cotton, catching the end of the rosette
chain to hold it. Work buds at top of spikes in
twisted chain stitch.
2. Sew a bead in the centre of each flower.
3. Work stems in whipped chain stitch.

Key

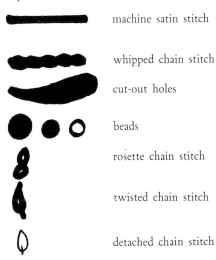

machine satin stitch

whipped chain stitch

cut-out holes

beads

rosette chain stitch

twisted chain stitch

detached chain stitch

Bows and Garlands

Ribbon embroidery can be used very effectively in lingerie, as shown by this nightdress yoke. When working on a sheer or very light coloured fabric take care that the ends of ribbons and threads are finished off so that they do not show through the fabric.

The design illustrated is worked on cotton voile. The quantities quoted are for the design as illustrated. The diagram is of the bow and garland only. The arrangement of these elements is left to the individual.

You will need
2 m of two close shades of 3 mm silk or soft
    polyester ribbon
stranded cotton to match the darker shade
perle cotton No. 8 to match the lighter shade
stranded cotton in three shades of contrast colour,
    and to match the fabric

Method
1. Take 0.5 m of each of the two shades of silk or polyester ribbon and tie a bow, using the two ribbons together.
2. Pin the double bow in place where required, pin out all parts, then baste.
3. Work stem stitch in one strand of stranded cotton along the edges of the darker ribbon.
4. Work French knots in perle cotton No. 8 down the centre of the lighter ribbon.
5. If using several bows in the design, make them and embroider in place.
6. With a sharp pencil mark a series of dots on the fabric along the centre line of the garland, between the bows.
7. Starting at the centre of the garland and using the deepest shade of the contrasting stranded cotton, work three pin roses—the centre rose should be slightly larger than the others. Follow

with one each side of these in the next shade, then two each side in the lightest shade. Work a French knot in the centre of each rose in perle cotton. 8. Using the two lighter shades of the roses work the rest of the garland in French knots, starting with six strands and graduating to three strands. Add French knots between the pin roses to fill out the garland.

The illustrated yoke has a line of French knots just inside the neckline and yoke, at the edge of the trimmed seam. This make an attractive finish.

Seams in sheer fabric should be narrowly trimmed and overcast, by hand or machine, or French seamed.

Key

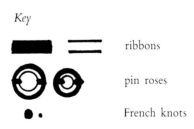

ribbons

pin roses

French knots

Green Daisies — Kath Chate

The embroidery on this jumper is worked over one shoulder and sleeve, both front and back.

The daisies are grouped very irregularly, no two groups quite the same, and are linked with continuous looping and curving lines.

Two shades of silk ribbon have been used for the daisies, which are worked in long detached chains, six to each flower. These stitches are worked over with a line of twisted chain stitch in a shiny thread in a similar colour to the ribbon.

The centres of the flowers are bullion knots worked in silk threads in colours to blend with the flowers. The continuous couched lines that link the groups of daisies are worked in either handspun silk or wool thread. The irregularities of the thread make a more interesting line than a smooth thread.

The colour of these lines is very close to that of the knitted jumper and does not make too great a contrast.

The illustration is of one group of daisies only. This type of design would not be difficult to work up and different flower forms could be used.

Key

chain stitch

twisted chain stitch

bullion knots

couching

Beaded Border

The centre of the design is 1.5 cm grey velvet ribbon ruched (see page 23). This is sewn down with sewing cotton as invisibly as possible.

Cretan stitch in grey 3 mm silk ribbon is worked either side of the velvet ribbon.

This is overlaid with Cretan stitch in pink perle cotton No. 5, catching in the edge of the velvet ribbon with some of the stitches.

More Cretan stitch, unevenly worked, spreads out from the row in perle cotton No. 5, this time in a fine sewing cotton (one strand of stranded cotton could be used).

The three different types of beads are a pink bugle bead, a silver short bugle bead and an oval grey pearl. These are sewn over and into the stitchery, with a few silver beads sewn to the ruched velvet ribbon.

This design would be suitable for an evening jacket, blouse or jumper.

To estimate the quantity of ribbon needed, measure the length of the border on the garment and double it for the velvet ribbon; double it again for the silk ribbon.

Beads are harder to estimate as they are sold in different ways, in packets, plastic containers or bunches usually. It is better to have a surplus than not enough.

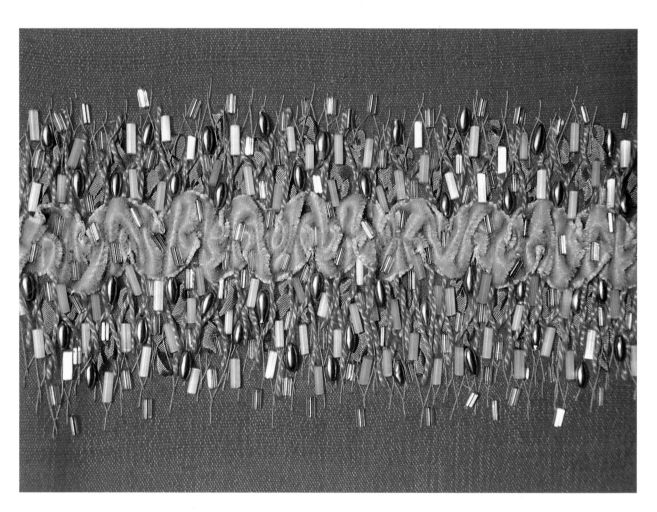

Zig-zag Border

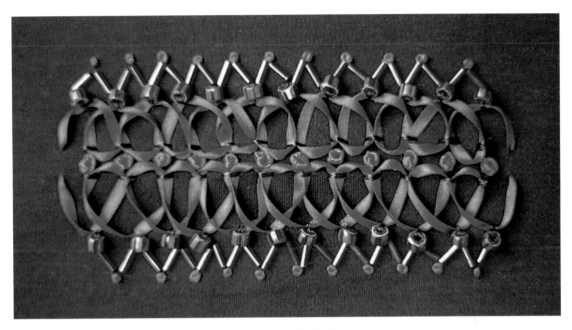

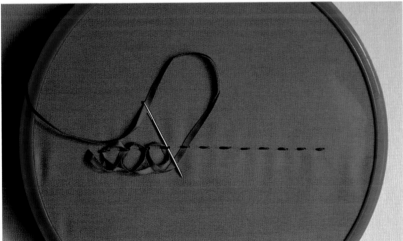

The example is worked on cotton jersey backed with calico.

The basis of the design is two rows of threaded running stitch 1 cm apart. The running stitches are about 5 mm long, with 5 mm between each stitch. Try to keep them even, and the loops the same length. When threading the ribbon through the stitches it must be kept lying the same way. If a new length of ribbon has to be joined, end and re-start under a running stitch.

Unusual striped beads hold down the loops of the ribbon, and two bugle beads have been sewn in a V between the striped beads. French knots in perle cotton No. 5 finish the edges.

Large French knots in polyester satin ribbon are worked down the centre of the design.

This design can be worked across a yoke or around the hem of a skirt, as a border around a jacket, or, working it vertically, up the front of a jacket.

When estimating the quantity of ribbon for the threading, measure the length the embroidery is to cover and multiply by four.

BAGS AND ACCESSORIES

Velvet Drawstring Bag
— Ethel Oates

Ethel Oates made this bag when she was over ninety years old.

To embroider it she used some of her store of lovely old shaded silk ribbons, kept since she worked ribbon embroidered items for her trousseau, as well as contemporary silk and polyester ribbons.

The design was inspired by a nineteenth century bag in the collection of The Embroiderers' Guild of Victoria, and incorporates many different flowers—roses and buds, violets, fuchsias and daisies. The stitches include detached chains, spider's webs, French knots, straight stitches and loops.

The rounded shape is very attractive and would be easy to make up. Two pieces, cut as the diagram and sewn together up to the casing line, with a lining cut and stitched the same, then inserted into the bag and the top and sides handsewn up to the casing. A casing can be hand or machine sewn with two lengths of ribbon threaded through for drawstrings.

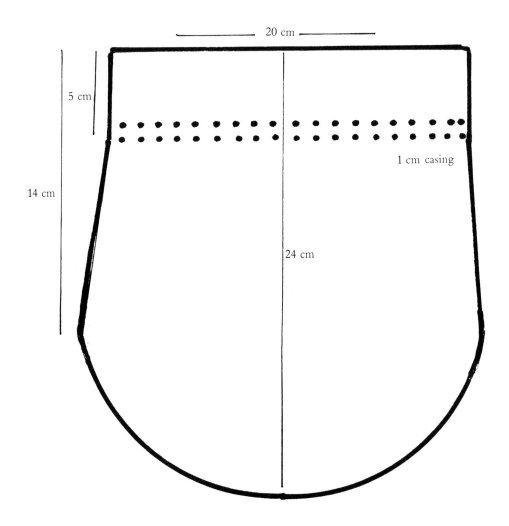

Key

Cretan stitch in ribbon

Cretan stitch in thread

beads

Evening Bag

This design involves the traditional Indian method of attaching small pieces of mirror called *shisha* to fabric. These can be bought at some needlework shops. Large sequins can be used in the same way.

You will need
velvet or velveteen 45 × 28 cm
lining fabric 45 × 28 cm
interfacing 45 × 28 cm
20 cm of 1.5 cm Velcro
45 cm of 7–8 cm ribbon
7 pieces of *shisha* or sequins
2 m of 3 mm silver ribbon
1 m of 1.5 mm satin ribbon
broder cotton to tone with the ribbon
stranded cotton to tone with ribbon and a soft
   contrasting colour
silver beads
1 m of 3 mm silk ribbon in a soft contrasting
   colour

Method
1. Working on the wide ribbon start with the largest circle in the design.
2. Attach the mirror or sequin as shown in the photograph. Work a circle of running stitches around it about 1 cm from the mirror.
3. Bring the silver ribbon through near the mirror and work Cretan stitch over the framework attaching the mirror and the running stitch around the mirror. This is instead of pulling the ribbon through the fabric. Take care to keep the ribbon flat while working the stitches. The end of the ribbon can be taken behind the mirror and then cut off.
4. Work groups of Cretan stitch, in two strands of stranded cotton in the contrasting colour, between the ribbon stitches.
5. Sew a bead at the end of each ribbon stitch.
6. Work two circles with mirrors and the 1.5 mm ribbon in the same manner, with groups of Cretan stitches in two strands of stranded cotton in a colour of the same tone as the ribbon. Sew a bead at the end of each ribbon stitch.
7. The other four circles are worked with mirrors and broder cotton to tone with the wide ribbon background. The circle at each end of the design

has Cretan stitch worked around it in one strand of stranded cotton in the contrasting colour. Sew beads around the four circles.

8. Circular groups of beads are sewn at intervals down each side of the design.

9. Centre the embroidered ribbon on the velveteen, baste it carefully into place, then sew each side to the velvet over the contrasting silk ribbon. It is easiest to tuck the silk ribbon under the wide ribbon as you sew it.

10. Sew a length of the silver ribbon at the side of the contrasting ribbon.

To make up

1. Cut the piece of interlining 1.5 cm smaller all round than the velvet.

2. Fold the velvet over the edge of the interfacing and sew down, taking care not to take the stitches through to the front.

3. Turn under the lining and sew neatly to the prepared velvet. Right sides together, fold up the end not embroidered to the required length for

the bag and sew each side firmly together. Turn right side out and press very carefully. Sew the Velcro fastening to the underside of the flap and to the bag.

Roses Evening Bag

The evening bag illustrated has a 1920s vintage frame and handle, and the design of the embroidery is related to the shape of the handle.

It is important when making a bag to consider any special use for it, and to include the handles in the design.

The bag is made in a polyester moiré taffeta.

This design could be adapted for a box top or for evening wear.

The quantities are for the diagram size illustrated.

You will need
fabric 20 × 40 cm
lining 20 × 40 cm
thin wadding 20 × 40 cm

0.5 m of 15 mm satin ribbon in a colour to tone with the fabric
1 m of 10 mm satin ribbon in a lighter shade
1 m of 10 mm velvet ribbon to match the fabric
1.5 m of 3 mm silk or polyester ribbon in a contrasting colour
sewing cotton to match the ribbons and fabric
perle cotton No. 8 in a similar tone to the velvet ribbon
small silver or gold beads

Method
1. Mark the lines of the edge of the design on the fabric with a water soluble fabric marking pen or a line of basting. Mark the placement of the three roses.
2. Make a wound rose in the centre of the design in the 15 mm satin ribbon (see page 27). Sew beads in the centre.

3. Make two wound roses in the 10 mm satin ribbon each side of the centre. Sew beads in the centre.

4. With the velvet ribbon, make two bunches of three loops approximately 4 cm long. Sew the ends together, then place them just under the edge of the central rose and sew in place, sewing the loops here and there as invisibly as possible. Make two single loops and sew at the tops of the outer roses.

5. Work spider's webs in perle cotton.

6. Work French knots around the spider's webs in the silk or polyester ribbon.

7. Start the beading at the edges of the design. Attach each bead with a back stitch (see diagram on page 23). Continue beading in rows in brick fashion until the ground of the design is completely covered.

8. Line and interline the bag with the thin wadding and lining.

9. Most bag mounts and handles have holes in them along the edges and the bag can be attached to the mount through these. Use strong thread to match the bag and use a running stitch through the bag and holes. When this is completed, sew back to the start in between the previous stitches. Ribbon can be threaded through these stitches to make an attractive finish.

Key

wound rose   ribbon loop   spider's web   French knot   beads

Flower Basket Bag — Doris Waltho

This delightful and unusual bag would make a charming accessory for a bridesmaid or highlight an evening outfit.

The embroidery is simple, comprising wound roses, spider's webs, cross stitches, detached chains and French knots. These are worked in various ribbons and threads, including handspun silk thread, silk, satin and gauze ribbons, knitting ribbon and perle cotton. The basket is worked in buttonhole stitch in shaded perle cotton No. 5, which is threaded with satin ribbon. The rows of buttonhole stitch are worked in brick fashion with the stitches fairly wide apart. The edges of the satin ribbon have been machine stitched to secure them. Each side of the bag is worked similarly, but not exactly the same, keeping the outside edges alike in shape so that the two halves of the bag will join together well.

The embroidered sides are folded over thin wadding, each lined separately, then the two sides joined together with ladder stitch, leaving an adequate opening. A Velcro spot makes a satisfactory fastening, placed in the centre of the opening.

The handle is of plaited ribbons in colours that appear in the embroidery.

Drawstring Evening Bag
— Effie Mitrofanis

This very glamorous evening bag is made of Thai silk.

The ribbon roses are made of the same silk cut in different widths and machined on the edges with a narrow zig-zag stitch, sometimes in gold thread.

Folded roses were constructed from these 'ribbons', some with bead tassels from the centres.

Stitchery with beads and sequins in a very free individual style makes this bag an original creation.

The stitches include bullion knots, Cretan stitch, French knots, buttonholed circles and straight stitches.

The 14 cm diameter circular base is constructed from three layers of Foamcore cardboard, covered with silk. The sides are a strip of fabric 90 × 32 cm, lined with the same fabric, gathered at the lower edge and hand sewn to the covered base. A casing is machine sewn 6 cm from the top edge, and a handmade twisted cord is used for the drawstrings.

Floral Stripe Bag

This design combines floral braid, ribbons, wooden beads, leather buttons and stitchery.

There are many beautiful floral braids available and variations on this striped design would not be difficult to work out.

The braid used in the illustration has been integrated with the ribbons by means of the stitchery around each flower. The gradation of colour in the threads makes a more interesting effect than if only one colour were used. Tote bags, cushions and clothing could be embroidered in a similar way.

The handbag illustrated measures 26.5 × 17 cm.

The embroidery was worked in a continuous strip on the front, back and flap.

The fabric is a lightweight canvas, lined with a cotton to match one of the ribbons in the embroidery.

You will need
lightweight canvas or heavy cotton 70 × 30 cm
cotton for lining 35 × 30 cm
3 m floral braid approximately 1.5 cm wide
3 m of 15 mm nylon ribbon to tone with one of the colours in the braid
3 m of 8 mm nylon ribbon in another colour
stranded cotton in three shades to tone with colours in the braid

10 × 2 cm diameter flat wooden 'spacer' beads
12 × 1.5 cm diameter buttons
3 m each of 3 mm silk or polyester ribbon in
    lighter shades of the colours of the two nylon
    ribbons
sewing cotton to match fabric, braid and ribbons
2 brass corners (optional)
2 pairs Velcro spots for fastening

Method

1. Decide on the spacing of the braid and ribbons and the width of the stripes the embroidery will form.
2. Pin the braids and ribbon to the fabric and machine stitch down both edges with a fairly small stitch. Always stitch in the same direction to avoid buckling the ribbon.
3. Sew on the beads and buttons where required and add simple stitches around them in the silk or polyester ribbon. Single chain stitches have been used on the bag illustrated.
4. With one strand of stranded cotton work Cretan stitch around flowers of the braid, carrying the stitch outside the braid and working it unevenly. Graduate the colours of the thread to tone with the colours in the braid.
5. Take 65 cm of the braid and the 15 mm nylon ribbon and machine stitch the braid to the ribbon, down both edges.
6. Machine stitch the lining right sides together to each end of the embroidered fabric, taking 1.5 cm turnings. Trim seams and press towards the lining.
7. Fold the fabric, right sides together, so that the lining section is at one end. The other end, with double canvas fabric, forms the flap of the bag.
8. Insert the prepared handle into the sides just above the lining and pin, making sure it is not twisted—it will be between the layers of fabric.
9. Machine stitch the sides, leaving an opening at the lining end large enough to turn the bag right side out. Trim seams.
10. Turn the bag right side out and press carefully. Make sure the lining does not extend beyond the edges of the bag. Turn the edges of the opening under and press, then slip stitch by hand.
11. Machine stitch along the edge of the end that is lined.
12. Fold this end up to the top of the lining and pin at the sides, then baste.
13. Machine stitch at the edge, down the sides of the bag and around the flap. Use a fairly large stitch.
14. Hand sew the Velcro spots in position at each side under the flap and corresponding places on the bag.
15. To attach brass corners to the flap, spread a little fabric glue into the groove of the corner with a needle, slip onto the fabric corner, then cover with a piece of scrap fabric and pinch together with pliers.

Haircombs

Haircombs can be decorated in a number of ways for day or evening wear. Bows, flowers, folded and ruched ribbon are all effective and could be used in endless permutations. The two combs illustrated are both very simple to make.

Comb with three roses

You will need
1 haircomb
75 cm of 22 mm satin ribbon
0.5 m of 35 mm satin ribbon
0.5 m of 15 mm satin ribbon (choose three tones of one colour)
sewing cotton to match the ribbons
3 diamanté beads

Method
1. Cut a piece of the 22 mm ribbon twice the width of the comb plus 2 cm.
2. Fold 1 cm of this ribbon to the back of one end of the top of the comb, then sew the ribbon to the outside of the comb through the prongs. Take care not to extend the ribbon down the prongs. If there is any surplus width of ribbon leave it at the top of the comb.
3. Make three folded roses with the three different ribbons, leaving tails on the two smaller ones.
4. Sew a diamanté bead to each flower.
5. Sew the roses to the comb through the ribbon.
6. Fold the other half of the ribbon attached to the comb to the back, turn in the cut edge and sew neatly together at both edges.

Comb with rosebuds and pearls

You will need
1 haircomb
20 cm of 15 mm velvet ribbon
0.5 m of 15 mm satin ribbon
0.5 m of 3 mm satin ribbon with a picot edge
15 cm each of 20 mm and 25 mm satin ribbon in two colours
about 16 pearls, preferably in graduated sizes

Method

1. Attach the velvet ribbon to the comb as described previously.
2. Fold the picot-edged ribbon into two bunches of loops of different lengths. Sew the ends together. Sew these to the comb through the velvet ribbon.
3. Make five rolled rosebuds, three in the 15 mm satin ribbon and one each in the other ribbons. Sew these to the comb over the bunches of loops.
4. Sew the pearls to the comb.
5. Fold the rest of the velvet ribbon to the back of the comb, turn in the end and sew neatly down both edges of the ribbon.

Hairslide

You will need

1 hairslide about 8 cm long
firm plastic 9 × 6 cm (plastic from an icecream carton is ideal)
fabric 20 × 8 cm
0.5 m of 15 mm satin ribbon
0.5 m of 1.5 mm satin ribbon in a light colour
0.5 m of 3 mm silk or polyester ribbon in another colour
0.5 m of 10 mm velvet ribbon
small silver or gold beads

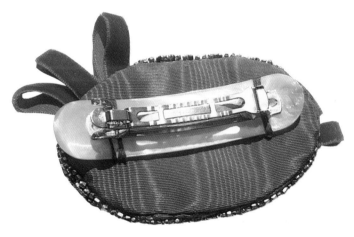

Method

1. Work a wound rose in the centre of half the fabric, sew beads in the centre.
2. Make two bunches of velvet ribbon loops as for the evening bag on page 61, and attach each side of the rose.
3. Add French knots in the 1.5 mm satin ribbon or silk or polyester ribbon.
4. Bead the ground, as for the evening bag on page 61.
5. Cut the plastic in an oval shape large enough to cover the hairslide.
6. Centre the embroidery over the plastic and run a gathering thread around it. Pull up firmly and fasten off.
7. Line the back with the same fabric, turning the edges under and sewing neatly.
8. Attach the hairslide to the back of the mounted embroidery, sewing it firmly where possible.

JEWELLERY

Beads

Fabric beads are easily made and embroidered. Combined with more conventional beads they make very unusual jewellery.

Three different necklaces are illustrated.

One is of large dark blue velvet beads embroidered in running stitch and threaded running stitch and threaded with crimson and mauve ribbons. These beads are combined with large grey pearl beads.

The second is of silk in four bright colours, embroidered with silk ribbons and glass and crystal beads, using chain stitch.

Another is of black satin with spider's web roses worked in cream satin ribbon and pearls.

You will need
enough fabric to cut on the bias for the number
   of beads you require
wadding
ribbons
sewing cotton to match the fabric and ribbons
beads
fishing line

Method
1. Cut a 6 cm wide strip of fabric on the bias.

2. Fold in half, right sides together, and machine stitch, taking in 0.5 cm seam.
3. Trim the seam and turn right side out. This tubing or rouleau is the basis for the beads.
4. Cut into lengths the size of the beads required, allowing an extra 1 cm for turnings. If making a necklace, cut all the bead lengths first, to get them a uniform size.
5. Take a piece of wadding approximately 5 × 10 cm and roll it tightly to make a 5 cm long roll.
6. Stuff this into the cut length of rouleau using a stuffing stick or the points of small scissors.
7. Turn in one end of the fabric at the end of the bead, and run a running stitch around it. Pull up firmly and fasten off. Repeat at the other end.
8. Decorate the bead. This is best done after the beads are made. Keep the embroidery as simple as possible. Threads and soft ribbons can be pulled through the ends of the fabric beads to start.

To make a spider's web on a bead, bring the thread for the groundwork through to the place required and work as usual. Thread the ribbon under the groundwork and stitch down. This is easier than pulling the ribbon through the fabric bead. When the web is completed take the ribbon under the groundwork again and sew down.

To thread the beads, take a length of fishing line approximately twice the finished length of the necklace and thread the beads on this. Glass, plastic or wooden beads can be threaded between the fabric beads.

You will need a large darning needle to thread the fabric beads; this will usually have to be un-threaded to thread the ordinary beads as they have a small hole.

If using a fastener, knot the fishing line very tightly several times to each end of the fastener, then thread back through at least two fabric beads before trimming.

Earrings can very easily be made and attached to hooks or clips obtained from craft shops.

Making a fabric bead

Brooches

These brooches can be initials, circles or any other simple geometric shape. The rich effect is obtained by using several tones of the same colour with a small amount of contrast, and by working the embroidery very densely.

First, on paper, draw the shape you have chosen exactly the size you require, then fill this shape with an arrangement of circles or ovals in different sizes.

H-brooch

You will need
fabric about 6 cm square (velveteen, satin, silk or
    heavy rayon)
0.5 m each of two tones of 3 mm wide silk or
    soft polyester ribbon
0.5 m each of two tones of 3 mm double-sided
    satin ribbon
perle cotton No. 5 in two tones similar to these
    ribbons
sewing cotton in a tone of these colours
0.5 m of 3 mm wide double-sided satin ribbon
    in a contrast colour
firm card or plastic 6 cm square
felt or leather for backing 6 cm square
brooch fastener (available from a lapidary supply
    shop)

Method
1. Mark the exact shape of the brooch on the fabric, using either a sharp pencil or a water soluble fabric marking pen.
2. Mark dots for the centres of the larger circles.
3. Work spider's webs over the dots using a variety of the four tones of 3 mm ribbons.
4. Add smaller spider's webs in perle cotton, then French knots in both ribbon and perle cotton to fill the spaces between the spider's webs.
5. Work small loops in the contrasting coloured ribbon last. These need to be well secured at the back of the work with sewing cotton.
6. Press the embroidery on the wrong side, on a well-padded surface.
7. Cut the card or plastic to the shape required with a craft knife. Lightly sandpaper the edges to smooth them.

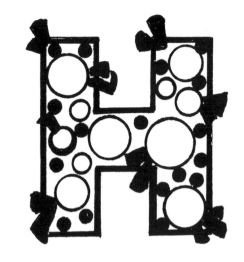

Key

spider's webs

French knots

loops

Key

○   detached chain

● ●   French knots

8. Cut a piece of felt or leather exactly the same size as the card. Cut the embroidered fabric 1.5 cm larger all round than the card shape. Carefully clip into corners and curves, allowing enough fabric to cover the card.

9. Spread a little glue onto the back of the card, then wrap the embroidery over the card and adhere to the back. Fold the corners over as neatly as possible. Use a darning needle to add spots of glue where needed.

10. Sew the brooch fastener to the felt or leather backing, which you have already cut out.

11. Glue the backing to the back of the brooch.

J-brooch

You will need
1 m each of 3 mm wide silk or soft polyester
    ribbon in three tones of the same colour
1 m double-sided satin ribbon in a bright colour
perle cotton No. 5 in a tone of the same colour
    as the satin ribbon, and in a contrasting colour
card or plastic 6 cm square
felt or leather for backing 6 cm square
brooch fastener

Method
1. Mark the shape of the brooch on the fabric with either a sharp pencil or a water soluble fabric marking pen.

2. Mark dots on the fabric where the groups of large French knots will be. Work chain stitches in semi-circles around these dots in the three tones of 3 mm wide ribbon.

3. Add French knots in the satin ribbon and one tone of the perle cotton.

4. Fill any spaces with French knots in perle cotton, adding the contrasting colour last.

    Make up as for the H-brooch.

Waratah Brooch and Bag

The waratah, a spectacular Australian native plant, is the floral emblem of New South Wales.

This brooch and its matching bag would make a charming gift for an overseas visitor or friend. It has been worked on velveteen with silk and satin ribbons and beads, both round and square ended.

Designs of other native flowers could be worked in a similar way.

You will need
velveteen 10 × 20 cm
fabric for lining 10 × 16 cm
thin wadding 10 × 16 cm
2 m each of two shades of 3 mm red silk ribbon
1 m each of two shades of 3 mm satin ribbon
red beads, both round and square ended, have been used in the illustrated set, but round beads only would be quite satisfactory
green stranded cotton
sewing cotton to match the velveteen and red satin ribbons
brooch mount
small piece of card the size of the brooch mount
fabric glue

Method
1. Cut two pieces of velveteen 10 × 8 cm.
2. On one of these pieces mark the outline of the three waratahs with a water soluble fabric marking pen, using a dotted line.
3. With the red silk ribbons work a few straight stitches to define the lower half of the waratahs, making this section a little over half of the shape. Use more of the darker shade of ribbon.
4. Make some twisted curls with the silk ribbons, over the straight stitches (see instructions for the chrysanthemum on page 24).
5. Bead the top half of the flowers, working the

outline first and then sewing the beads between the previous row, brick fashion.

6. Add two or three curls in silk ribbon, bringing them over the beaded section.

7. Make four or five straight stitches from the outside into the lower centre of the flower, using the red satin ribbons. Leave these stitches fairly loose, and twist them a little. Sew them in place with matching sewing cotton.

8. Work leaves in fly stitch with one strand of stranded cotton.

9. Work one waratah and leaves on the remaining velveteen for the brooch.

To make up the bag

1. Cut two oval shapes in the thin wadding, exactly the size of the bag. Cut the two pieces of velveteen, one embroidered, 1 cm larger.

2. Cut two oval pieces of lining fabric the same size.

3. Cover the wadding shapes with the velveteen. Gather around the curves to achieve a smooth finish.

4. Press lightly into a well padded surface.

5. Turn in the edge of the lining pieces and sew neatly to the prepared velveteen sides.

6. Sew the two sides of the bag together with ladder stitch, leaving an opening large enough to take the brooch.

7. Attach 20 cm of the red satin ribbon to each side of the bag at the centre of the opening, using both shades of ribbon, one on each side.

The bag illustrated fastens with a bow at the lower centre. This is deliberate, as the bow finishes the design and would look odd at the top.

To make up the brooch

1. Cut the card so that it will fit loosely into the brooch mount.

2. Cut the embroidered fabric for the brooch about 1 cm larger than the card and run a running stitch around the edge.

3. Centre the embroidery over the card, draw up the running stitch until the fabric fits firmly over the card. Fasten off securely.

4. Check to see that the covered card fits snugly in the mount, and make any adjustments.

5. Apply some glue to the back of the covered card, spread with a darning needle. Fit the embroidery into the mount and press firmly.

Key

● ● ●   beads

curls

twisted straight stitches

two rows of fly stitches

73

Beaded Pendant and Bag

A pendant with its own matching bag makes a very special gift. This idea can be used with other items of fabric jewellery. The bag can be related to the jewellery by the materials, colour, design or combinations of these elements.

Pendant

You will need
silk approx. 9 × 10 cm
1 m each of 3 mm silk or polyester ribbon in two
    colours
sewing thread to match the fabric
0.5 m of 1.5 mm satin ribbon
card or plastic 9 × 10 cm
small glass beads in three or four colours to tone
    with the fabric and ribbons
stranded cotton to tone with one of the colours
    of the beads
chain or enough ribbon to hang the pendant
3 large beads in a contrast colour
fabric glue
suede, felt or thin leather 9 × 10 cm

Method
1. Mark the central shape on the fabric with pencil dots.
2. At the centre of this shape work a small spider's web in one of the silk ribbons.
3. Bead solidly around the spider's web to the edge of the shape.
4. With the other silk ribbon work a row of small loops around the beaded shape.
5. Attach each loop to the fabric with a bead.
6. Work a row of single chain stitches in two strands of stranded cotton around the row of loops, putting a bead at the end of each stitch.

To make up
1. Cut the card or plastic to the shape of the pendant.
2. Fold the embroidered fabric over this and glue to the back.
3. Glue a small loop of ribbon to the top of the pendant and a tassel of beads and ribbons to the lower centre.
4. Cut a piece of suede, felt or thin leather a fraction smaller than the pendant and glue to the back.

Bag

You will need
velvet 30 × 15 cm
lining 30 × 15 cm
thin wadding 30 × 30 cm
1 m each of two colours of 3 mm silk or polyester
    ribbon
1 m of 3 mm satin ribbon
2 m of 1.5 mm satin ribbon
beads in the same colours as the pendant
stranded cotton to match the velvet
15 large beads in a contrast colour

Method
1. Cut the piece of velvet into two pieces 15 ×
15 cm.
2. In the centre of one piece sew seven large beads
in a circle with one in the centre.

Key

O ᴑ ₒ beads

O spider's web

▌ ▐ ᵠ chain stitches

● French knot

3. Work single chains around this in satin ribbon.

4. Work French knots in six strands of stranded cotton between these stitches and the beads.

5. Work two more rows of single chains in silk ribbon, working them between the previous row.

6. Sew a bead with a circle of beads around it at the end of the satin ribbon chains.

7. Sew a bead at the end of each other chain.

To make up

1. Cut four pieces of thin wadding the exact shape of the bag.

2. Cut the embroidered velvet and lining 1.5 cm larger.

3. Fold each piece of velvet and each piece of lining over a cut shape of wadding and stitch by hand, taking care not to take the stitches through to the front.

4. Sew the lining to each half of the outside of the bag, sewing it just inside the outside edge with a slip stitch.

5. Sew the two halves of the bag together with ladder stitch. Leave an opening at the top large enough to take the pendant easily.

6. Sew two lengths of fine ribbon to each side of the top of the bag, sewing the ribbons in the centre. Thread beads onto the ribbons and knot.

Chrysanthemum Brooch and Bag

The chrysanthemums are worked in silk ribbons on moiré taffeta with gold beads making rich centres to the flowers.

The bag can be used as a container for the brooch or for other jewellery such as chains or pearls. It can also be used as a cosmetic purse.

You will need
fabric 42 × 24 cm
thin wadding 36 × 12 cm
4 m each of two close shades of silk ribbon 3 mm
    wide
perle cotton No. 8 for stems and leaves
gold beads
sewing thread to match the fabric
oval brooch mount (obtainable at craft shops)
fabric glue

Method

1. Cut 6 cm off the length of the fabric. This will be for the brooch.

2. Press the fabric in half lengthwise, making a piece 12 × 36 cm.

3. Open out and at the centre of the right hand side of one end and about 9 cm in, mark in pencil dots an oval the size of the large chrysanthemum, with another small oval for the centre of the flower. Mark dotted lines for the stems.

4. Work curled petals (see diagram on page 25)

in the two shades of silk ribbon, working a section at a time. Make straight stitches in twisted ribbon at the back of the flower.

5. Fill the centre with beads, and sew some around the flower.

6. Work the profile flower and bud in short curls, adding beads outside.

7. With perle cotton No. 8 work the stems and leaves in stem stitch.

To make up

1. Place a piece of wadding 34 × 9 cm on the wrong side of one half of the fabric.

2. Turn the fabric over the wadding and press.

3. Fold the other half of the fabric onto the padded side, turn under the seam allowances to match and press.

4. Ladder stitch around the edges.

5. Fold one-third of the length up and oversew the sides with neat small stitches with matching thread.

Brooch

1. Cut an oval of thin card slightly smaller than the size of the brooch.

2. Work a chrysanthemum on the fabric, in a size that will fill the shape of the brooch.

3. Cut the embroidered fabric 1 cm larger than the card.

4. Run a running stitch around the edge, centre the embroidery over the card, pull up firmly and fasten off securely.

5. Fit the embroidery into the brooch mount to see that it fits well. Make any adjustments.

6. Glue the embroidery into the mount with fabric glue.

Key

chrysanthemum petal

beads

stem stitch

Wattle Brooch and Bag

A design from another Australian shrub makes this delightful brooch and bag set.

The design is illustrated on a polyester and cotton fabric in silk ribbons, beads and stranded cotton and the bag is lined with silk.

You will need
fabric 22 × 10 cm
lining fabric 20 × 10 cm
thin wadding 20 × 10 cm
1 m of 3 mm green silk or soft polyester ribbon
yellow beads
green and yellow stranded cotton
0.5 m of 1.5 mm green satin ribbon
brooch mount
card the size of the mount
fabric glue
sewing cotton to match the fabric

Method
1. From the fabric cut two shapes for the bag, allowing 1 cm turnings.
2. On both pieces mark a series of dots, in pencil or water soluble fabric marking pen, following the central line of the design as illustrated.
3. Work the wattle flowers in beads, adding French knots at the ends of the sprays in three strands of stranded cotton.
4. Work straight stitches in the green silk ribbon.
5. Work fly stitches in one strand of stranded cotton around the straight stitches.
6. Work the design on the remaining fabric for the brooch.

To make up the brooch
Follow the instructions for the waratah brooch (page 73).

To make up the bag

1. Follow the instructions for the waratah bag (page 73). Sew the two halves of the bag together, leaving a section at the top to form the flap.

2. Sew a small loop of satin ribbon to the centre of the flap and a 22 cm length of the same ribbon to the front to correspond to the loop. Thread one end of this ribbon through the loop and tie a bow.

Key

● ● ●   beads

• • •   French knots

⟋   straight stitch

Y Y   fly stitch

PICTURES

Flower Picture *(28 × 21 cm, including mount)*

The types of flowers that can be worked in ribbon vary enormously. You may like to design your own picture, using some of the ideas for flowers in this book.

For a picture similar to the one illustrated, you will need
fabric about 30 × 25 cm in a neutral colour—velveteen, firm silk, rayon and linen or linen and polyester are all suitable (the picture illustrated is worked on linen and polyester)
1 m of 1 cm velvet ribbon
0.5 m of 3 mm satin ribbon to tone with the velvet ribbon
2 m of shaded knitting ribbon, or 3 mm wide soft ribbon in two shades
1.5 m of 5 mm single-sided satin ribbon
2 m each of two shades of 3 mm silk or soft polyester ribbon
2 m of 3 mm silk or soft polyester ribbon in a contrasting colour
perle cotton in two shades of green and a shade to tone with the contrasting coloured ribbon
stranded cotton in three shades of green and two shades of the colour chosen for the three sprays at the top of the design

Method
1. Work the largest flowers first. In the design illustrated these are the velvet ribbon flowers, worked in straight stitches, the stitches being left fairly loose. Work a French knot in the centre of each flower in 3 mm satin ribbon.
2. Next, work detached chain stitches between the velvet petals, using silk or soft polyester ribbon.
3. The groups of roses are worked in shaded knitting ribbon or soft ribbon in two shades.
4. Work a cluster of French knots in the single-sided satin ribbon.
5. Groups of small flowers in a contrasting colour are worked next, using silk or soft polyester ribbon in a straight cross stitch.
6. Another cross stitch in perle cotton is worked over the ribbon stitch.

7. The two sprays in knitting ribbon or soft ribbon are worked with twisted chain stitch.
8. The three sprays at the top of the design are worked in detached chain stitches, starting with narrow stitches in two strands of stranded cotton, then adding detached chain stitches in silk or polyester ribbon.
9. Three groups of three detached chains are next, using silk or soft ribbon in the same colour as the stitches between the velvet petals.
10. The leaves are detached chains, worked one inside the other and in groups. Use perle cotton.
11. Other leaves are worked in fly stitch, making stithces one underneath the other in groups of three or four, again in perle cotton.
12. The soft background around the flower posy is worked with fly stitches with long tails, in one strand of stranded cotton. Work in three shades, using the darkest colour at the base of the design, and the lightest around the top.
13. French knots in silk or soft polyester ribbon are scattered among the fly stitches.
14. The picture can be framed as it is or a fabric-covered mount added before framing.

To frame the picture you will need
cardboard, preferably acid-free, the size to fit the frame
fabric glue

Method
1. Centre the embroidery on the cardboard, making sure the weave of the fabric is straight. Place face down on a soft clean surface, such as a towel.
2. Cut a small amount of fabric from each corner, leaving enough to fold over the corners to the back of the card (see diagram).
3. Using fabric glue stick down first the corners, then the top and bottom, then the sides. The corners should be mitred, as shown in the diagrams, and sometimes need to be sewn to get a really neat finish.

Key

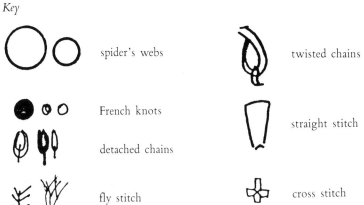

spider's webs

twisted chains

French knots

straight stitch

detached chains

fly stitch

cross stitch

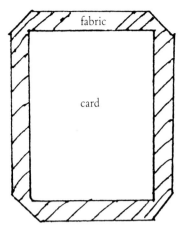

1

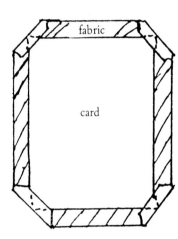

2

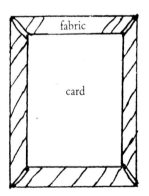

3

To make a fabric-covered mount you will need
fabric 5 cm larger all round than the mounted
 picture
card the same size as the picture
fabric glue

Method
1. Cut the centre out of the card to the shape desired. Pre-cut mounts can be bought from framing suppliers, and these save a lot of time and trouble.
2. Cover the mount in the same way as for the picture. Then cut the centre from the fabric, leaving a 2 cm turning.
3. Clip carefully into corners or around curves.
4. Spread a small amount of glue onto the back of the mount, around the central hole.
5. Carefully fold the fabric over the edge of the centre of the mount, and adhere this to the back of the mount.
6. The mount can then be glued over the picture, taking care not to have any glue too near the centre edge. Accidental glue spots can sometimes be removed by lifting off the glue with a needle. This needs to be done before the glue sets.

Seasons Remembered

These embroideries are a nostalgic remembrance of the seasons of my childhood in England. They are not specific places, but scenes from the mind's eye, romantic and evocative.

The four embroideries that make the set are all worked on dyed fabric. The dye used is one sold for screen printing on fabric; the colours mix together and are easily diluted with water. The dye is set with a hot iron.

In all the pieces the dye has been applied with a fairly large artist's paintbrush to wet fabric, letting the colours blend into one another to give a very soft effect.

When using dye on fabric as the basis for an embroidery, avoid the tendency to paint a picture. Only the suggestion of the background is necessary.

The four pieces are all mounted with velvet mounts and framed in 1930s vintage frames which were repainted to suit each piece.

Spring *(12 × 15 cm, embroidery only)*

The subject is a bluebell wood, looking out to a landscape of hills. I wanted to capture the fresh yellow-green of new beech leaves and the hazy blue of the bluebells.

The cotton fabric was painted with dye in blues and yellow-greens to suggest the areas of sky, trees and bluebells.

The hills were worked first in lines of stem stitch in one strand of stranded cotton. A hedge was suggested by ruched silk ribbon in a dark yellow-green (see page 23).

Satin ribbon and some fine rayon braid were stitched down over the landscape to start the tree trunks. These were stitched over with Cretan stitch and straight stitches in one strand of stranded cotton in several shades of grey and soft fawn. The ends of the braid were deliberately frayed and stitched down. Straight stitches in green silk ribbon, worked horizontally, were the basis for the leafy tree tops, and straight stitches in satin and silk ribbons worked vertically for the bluebells.

The blue stitches were made shorter as they went into the hills, to suggest distance. The areas of foliage and bluebells were then stitched all over in Cretan stitch, using one strand of stranded cotton and working the stitch horizontally for the foliage and vertically for the bluebells.

Many shades of green, yellow and blue were used, with brighter colours to the front of the picture.

Using many tones of colour will always give a rich effect, and the contrast of dull and shiny materials adds to this effect. Note that the stitchery is deliberately uneven, making the soft texture required.

Summer *(18 × 14 cm, embroidery only)*

The scene is part of a public park, with lawns, avenues of trees, a lake and beds of flowers.

The cotton calico was dyed as before, ruched ribbon was sewn in a line to suggest bushes and manipulated into fan shapes for small trees. The ribbon was stitched down and then embroidered over with French knots and chain stitches.

Short pieces of dark green ribbon were sewn down horizontally where the conifers were to be and these were stitched over with several shades of cotton using Cretan stitch worked horizontally. Some long straight stitches were added last to give direction to the trees.

The lake was worked with a shaded knitting ribbon stitched down as invisibly as possible, and then broken lines of stem stitch in fine thread were added.

The flower beds in the foreground were suggested by a gathered length of striped gauze ribbon, stitched over with bullion knots in reds and fly stitch in greens in perle cotton No. 8.

There are also chain stitches in green silk ribbon and French knots in various threads in bright pinks.

The overhanging tree is worked in single chain stitches in ribbons and various threads in copper colours.

The mount is light blue velvet.

Autumn (12 × 14 cm, embroidery only)

What I wanted to convey in this piece was a garden, rich with the colours of dahlias, dead leaves, woody stalks, shrubs turning colour and some bare trees.

The trees in the background were worked first, on dyed calico. Many shades of grey and soft pink in fine silk and one strand of stranded cotton were used in fly stitch and Cretan stitch, worked very unevenly, with the colours overlapping and in directions to form a tree shape.

Under these trees several rows of a shaded knitting ribbon were sewn down and stitched over with long detached chain stitches in two strands and one strand of stranded cotton, in colours similar to but darker than the trees.

The top part of the flower bed is composed of ruched shaded knitting ribbon, sewn down with fly stitches, with French knots added into it in similar colours and a golden yellow.

Straight stitches in various ribbons in mauves, reds and apricot form the background for feather stitch and fly stitch in similar colours and deeper tones in threads of various thickness.

French knots in several shades of golden yellow have been added at the edge of this area.

The foreground is composed of running stitches in perle cotton No. 5, threaded with silk ribbon in a circular direction, the colours varying from dark red to bright pink.

French knots in satin ribbon, handspun silk and perle cotton No. 5 are worked among the ribbons.

A flat area of shaded ribbon, sewn down with patches of Cretan stitch, forms the lower edge. On the right hand side, there is a small section of green silk ribbon in single chains, overlaid with chains in golden yellow fine thread.

The mount is dusty pink velvet.

Winter (20 × 15 cm, embroidery only)

This is a snow scene in the country, just before dusk, when the light sometimes has a pink tinge and there is the threat of more snow.

The cotton fabric was dyed mauve-grey and pink, leaving most of the foreground undyed to give the impression of snow.

The line of the hills in the distance was worked first, in stem stitch with fine silk thread in a soft grey.

The trees in the background were worked in straight stitches and fly stitches in ribbon and threads in greys and soft browns.

The line of trees in the middle distance have silk and satin ribbons as the basis of the trunks, stitched over with perle cotton No. 5 and stranded cotton in greys and browns, using straight stitches.

The hedge has a background of cross stitches in soft ribbon with overlaid stitches in perle cotton No. 8 and stranded cotton.

The gate is worked with stranded cotton in long stitches caught down with sewing cotton.

The tracks to the gate are running stitches in fawn stranded cotton.

The plant forms in the foreground are straight and fly stitches in satin ribbon, perle cotton No. 5 and stranded cotton.

'Winter' has a grey velvet mount.

Florist's Window

(16 × 27 cm, embroidery only)

The floor and shelf areas have been covered with dull grey-green taffeta, bonded to the linen background with fusible web. The details have been machine stitched, including the basket which is machined in rows of an automatic pattern. The flower containers are of black non-woven interfacing, black satin and green cotton. These fabrics have had fusible web bonded to them, been cut into the required shapes, then bonded to the background and machine stitched around the edges.

Bonding fabrics together with fusible web is a very easy form of appliqué and gives a very neat, clean outline.

The flowers in each container have been treated differently and make use of ribbons and hand stitchery. Some are ruched ribbon, some chain stitches, some loops of ribbon, others are in Cretan stitch, straight stitches and fly stitches. The shades of colour and contrast of dull and shiny materials give the work richness and depth.

Jibbon Beach (20 × 15 cm, embroidery only)

Jibbon Beach in Sydney's south is portrayed on a summer day. The colours of the sky, water, sand and foliage have been intensified to give the impression of strong light.

Washes of blue and yellow dye were painted onto wet cotton fabric to define the areas of sea, sand and sky. The strip of coastal area was worked first with various ribbons, folded and ruched, then stitched to the fabric.

Cretan stitch in a variety of threads was worked irregularly into and around the ribbons.

A line of stem stitch defines the edge of the sand and the tide line; the figures on the beach were worked in straight stitches.

The boat was cut out of non-woven interfacing and the details drawn on it in pencil. It was stitched down with long stitches which give the effect of shadow.

Golden yellow silk ribbon and narrow braid were laid in long straight stitches to start the rocky area. This was stitched over with stem stitch in perle cotton.

The flying seagulls are fly stitches in white perle cotton and the static gulls are single twisted chain stitches.

The embroidery is mounted in a series of four fabric covered mounts of different widths in the colours of sand, sky, birds and trees. The proportion of each colour in the mount is roughly the same as in the embroidery, highlighting and accentuating the colours of the beach scene.

Autumn in Bright, Victoria — Doris Waltho

(33 × 20 cm, embroidery only)

This colourful picture is a beautiful blend of applied fabrics, dyeing and hand stitchery in both ribbons and threads in great variety.

The basic fabric is calico, dyed to define the areas of path and trees. The dye was applied to wet fabric to get a very soft effect.

The area of the trees was overlaid with pieces of sheer cotton and organza to strengthen the colours. The tree tops were then stitched over with running stitches in silk ribbons, some satin ribbon, and many different threads, from quite heavy handspun silk thread to very fine stranded silk and cotton. The direction of the stitches and the range of colour, from dark wine red to pale apricot and lime green, gives the impression of autumn leaves.

The tree trunks are velvet ribbon, with raised stem band worked along one edge, the other edge sewn with either back stitch or stem stitch.

Stem stitch also forms the pathway, in fine silk threads and stranded cotton in shades of cream, white and grey. Note how many shades are used, with the stronger colour to the foreground to give the work perspective. The areas of fallen leaves are worked in running stitch with stranded cottons and silks in colours similar to the leaves of the trees, but the lighter texture gives this area good definition.

The work has been framed with a triple mount. The yellow, tan and fawn mount boards add to the colour effect and the touch of gold on the wood frame gives a pleasing finish.

The Yellow Garden — *Kath Chate*

(62 × 70 cm, including mount)

This garden scene combines appliqué with machine and hand embroidery in ribbons and threads. It is worked on a wool fabric and the applied materials include velvet, wool, silk, cotton and voile. The simple shapes of the trees and shrubs in the background are applied with freely worked machine embroidery. The tones of green blend with the wool ground, and are not too dominating, giving the effect of distance. A path is suggested by ovals of wool fabric stitched by hand with wool thread.

Of the two groups of flower shapes in fabric, one consists of bonded silks and cottons cut into irregular hexagons and sewn down in the centre with groups of small French knots. The other, paler flowers are circles of voile and silk gathered around the edge and pulled up, then turned over and sewn down with a large French knot at the centre.

Both these groups of flowers are rather three-dimensional and stand well away from the background.

The delightful hand stitchery is a very good example of the use of simple stitches in a variety of materials.

Fly, stem, chain, Cretan and straight stitches are worked in satin and silk ribbons, crewel wool and perle cotton. The crewel wool stitchery softens the effect of the shiny satin ribbons, achieving a subtle blend of colour and texture.

The line of continuous couching in heavy handspun wool suggests more shrubs and clumps of plants at the lower edge of the picture. The movement of this line is echoed by the unusually shaped mount which draws the eye into the focal area of yellow flowers.

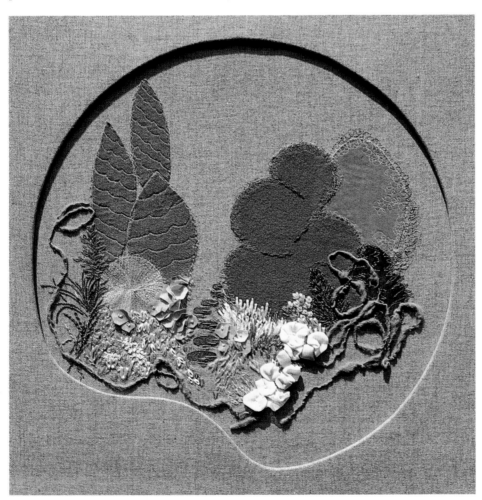

Flowers — *Doris Waltho*
(20 cm diameter, embroidery only)

This simple arrangement of flowers is an inspiration for a beginner, as the stitches are basic and easily achieved.

The background fabric is an openweave linen through which the ribbons can be pulled without difficulty.

There are spider's web roses, daisies in straight stitches, groups of fly stitch flowers, French knots and triangular flowers composed of a large detached chain with two more chains coming out of it. Another flower is a large detached chain with a straight stitch threaded under the tail of the chain.

All the ribbons are polyester satin in 2 mm and 3 mm widths.

Leaves and stems are in chain stitches, worked in a variety of threads. Wool, cotton, handspun silk and flower thread make a soft matt texture that complements the shiny, bright flowers.

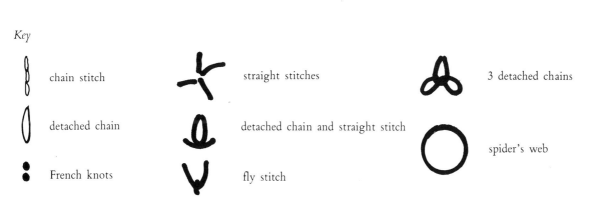

Key

8	chain stitch	⅄	straight stitches	♧	3 detached chains
❍	detached chain	♈	detached chain and straight stitch	◯	spider's web
⦂	French knots	ⱴ	fly stitch		

Wallflowers (11 × 17 cm)

This piece was inspired by a bed of wallflowers in a public park. The rich and rather unusual blend of colours was what appealed most.

The background fabric is a green shot silk.

The trees and bushes in the distance are organza which has been bonded to the silk with fusible web.

Details have been stitched with straight stitches.

The wallflowers are also worked in straight stitches in a variety of ribbons—silk, satin and rayon.

The blending of the colours was a fascinating experience and most enjoyable.

Favourite Flowers — Doris Waltho

(23 × 19 cm)

This delightful picture is created with stitchery in a combination of ribbons, handspun silk thread, suede thonging and stranded cotton on a wool background.

The velvet ribbon flowers are the focal point and consist of straight stitches, left rather loose, with French knots in satin ribbon at the centres.

The mauve flower spikes are worked in straight stitches in two shades of polyester satin ribbon, with detached chain stitches in three strands of stranded cotton worked amongst the ribbon.

Foliage is suggested by Cretan stitch in green satin ribbon, handspun silk thread and suede thonging. The direction of these stitches gives the piece life and movement.

It is framed in an oval green mount and a gold frame.

Basket of Flowers

(24 × 29 cm, embroidery only)

Baskets of flowers have been a favourite subject for the decorative arts for centuries, appearing in paintings, tapestries, fabrics and porcelains. These are wonderful sources of inspiration for ribbon embroidery.

It is always best to make a drawing of the design first. This does not have to be realistic—use circles and ovals for flowers. The important thing is to get the proportion right, and in this case the basket needs to be well thought out.

Transfer as little as possible to the fabric. The outline of the basket was the only part transferred in this piece. A piece of paper was cut out in the shape of the basket, pinned to the fabric and a line of pencil dots drawn around it. Once the outline is established the other lines follow easily.

The basket was worked first, in 3 mm polyester satin ribbon, sewn onto the lines of the basket with tiny stitches about every 3 cm. Then the top and bottom rows were woven through the first lines and stitched down. All the ribbon was then herringbone stitched with fine matching sewing cotton.

Twisted ribbon forms the other lines in the basket, making one twist at a time and stitching it down under the twist.

The second step is the ribbon and bow.

Take about 1.5 m of 6 mm satin ribbon. Cut it in half and tie one end over the edge of the basket. Pin in place, then sew the ribbon down with stem stitch along each edge, using one strand of stranded cotton in a matching colour. Attach the other half of the ribbon in the same way, taking it about 3 cm from the edge of the basket.

Tie a bow where the lines of ribbon meet and arrange and pin the bows and tails, then stitch down with stem stitch on each edge.

Using your drawing as a guide, work the larger flowers first: the gathered roses, carnations, spider's webs and iris. Fit daisies, lavender and forget-me-nots around them, then add rosebuds, periwinkle trails and French knot spikes.

The fine spikes of flowers are worked in one strand of stranded cotton, using tiny twisted chains for the flowers and stem stitch for the central stem.

The ferny leaves are also worked in one strand of stranded cotton, using fly stitches worked one underneath the other.

Flower stems in the basket are in stem stitch and twisted silk ribbon.

CUSHIONS

Lace and Ribbon Cushion

Lace, ribbons, threaded stitches and roses combine to make a rich texture on this wide band of embroidery. This example was worked on calico but linen, firm cotton or velveteen would also be suitable. The cushion can be finished with a frill of fabric or lace or both, and a zip fastener at the back is recommended.

The cushion illustrated measures 45 cm square, excluding frill.

You will need
75 cm fabric 115 cm wide—this includes a frill of single fabric (add another 25 cm if frill is to be double fabric)
1.5 m of 3 cm coarse cotton lace—this is for the cushion only (add 3.5 m for a lace frill)
2 m of 10 mm velvet ribbon
2 m of 5 mm picot-edged satin ribbon
3 m of 3 mm satin ribbon
3 m of 1.5 mm satin ribbon
3 m of 15 mm satin ribbon
(all these ribbons to be in different shades of the same colour)
6 m of 3 mm cream satin ribbon to match lace
perle cotton No. 8 in cream and main colour
sewing cotton in cream and main colour

Method
1. Cut a piece of fabric 48 cm square. Zig-zag by machine around the edge.
2. Hand sew a strip of lace down the centre, and a strip 5.5 cm each side of the central strip.
3. Work spider's webs at regular intervals down the centre of each strip of lace, using cream satin ribbon. Use the pattern of the lace as a guide.
4. Work four rows of running stitch in cream perle cotton about 5 mm from each side of the lace strips and thread with 3 mm satin ribbon in one of the main shades. Don't pull the ribbon too tightly.
5. Next, tack a strip of the picot-edged ribbon beside the threaded running stitch. Attach it to the fabric by working French knots through each

picot in perle cotton, using cream and the main colour alternately.
6. Now tack a length of 10 mm velvet ribbon down the centre of the space between the picot-edged ribbon.
7. Attach it to the fabric with detached chains in perle cotton, about 1.5 cm apart.
8. Then work a row of running stitches using perle cotton in the main colour, just inside the detached chains. Thread this with the 1.5 mm satin ribbon.
9. Make two sets of double loops in velvet ribbon and sew diagonally across the velvet stripes.
10. Make six folded roses from the 15 mm satin ribbon and sew in two groups of three to the centre of the velvet loops.

To make up
1. Cut a piece of fabric 48 × 51 cm.
2. Cut this in half across the 51 cm length, and sew in a zip fastener to join the halves together, taking in 1.5 cm seams.
3. Round off the corners of the embroidered side of the cushion. Cut, hem and gather the frill and tack around edge.
4. Place the back and front right sides together, with the zip opened, and stitch around the edge. Trim the seam and overcast with zig-zag or by hand.
5. Turn right side out and press carefully.

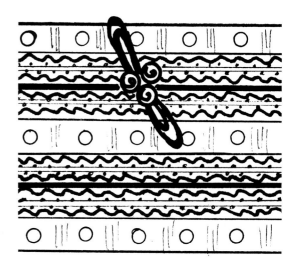

Key

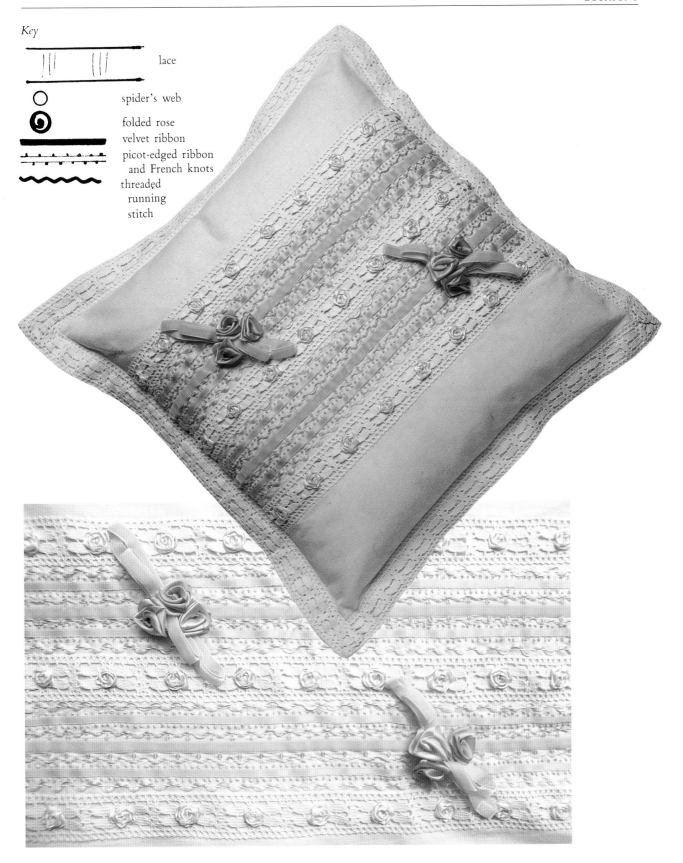

lace

spider's web

folded rose

velvet ribbon

picot-edged ribbon
and French knots

threaded
running
stitch

Round Cushions — *Kath Chate*

These circular cushions have been embroidered very freely with ribbons, both silk and polyester, handspun silk threads, perle cotton, flower thread and fine silk thread.

Detached chain and fly stitches are worked in the various ribbons and perle cottons, the colours blending in graduated sections of colour.

Freely worked Cretan stitch softens some of the heavy stitchery.

The direction of the stitchery gives movement, and strong lines of double knot stitch on one cushion add to the effect.

Although the cushions are different, the colours, circular shape and stitches make them a pair.

Other stitches include feather stitch, French knots and twisted chain stitch.

The cushions are worked on a wool fabric.

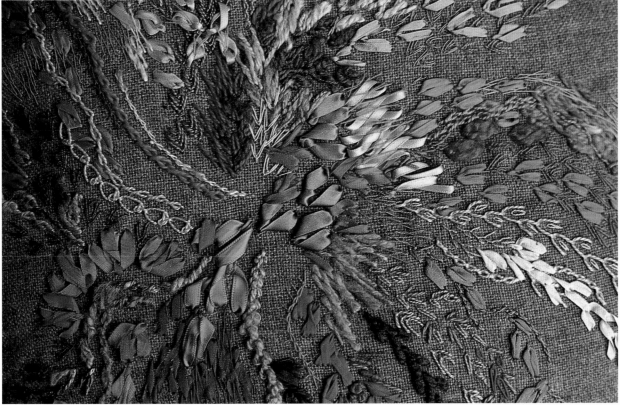

CARDS

Small embroideries make very personal and attractive cards and can be designed especially for an individual or a special occasion.

The cards illustrated here give a few ideas.

Cards specially made for use with embroidery can be bought at many embroidery and craft shops, while Ingres paper, handmade paper, thin cardboard and heavy cartridge paper are all suitable for making your own cards.

Sometimes it is a good idea to put a piece of thin wadding behind the embroidery before glueing the cardboard over the back. This is especially useful with fine silk fabrics.

Knot Flower Cards

Here is a way to use those leftover lengths of ribbon. Simply tie them in knots, singly or several together, and sew them to fabric. Add some fine ribbon stalks to make an attractive bunch of flowers.

This idea can be used on clothing, bags and small pictures, either using the knot flowers on their own or with other ribbon flowers.

Cards are easy and quick to make.

You will need
lightweight, coloured cardboard 30 × 14 cm
fabric 8 × 12 cm
several short lengths of coloured ribbons (4–5 cm long)
short lengths of green ribbon
sewing cotton
fabric glue

Method
1. Tie the short lengths of ribbon in knots.
2. Arrange the knot flowers on the fabric and sew down carefully. Sew on the stalks.
3. On the inside of the cardboard, mark two lines 10 cm from each end of the 30 cm length. Fold inwards on these lines. Out of the centre panel cut a window 6 × 10 cm. This leaves a border of 2 cm all round.
4. With fabric glue, stick the embroidered fabric over the window. Always put the glue on the card, and not too near the edge.
5. Trim a fraction off the end of the card at the left of the back of the embroidery.
6. Lightly glue this side around the edge *only*, and press over the back of the embroidery.
7. Fold firmly down the other fold. It helps to place cards under a book for a short while, to flatten them.

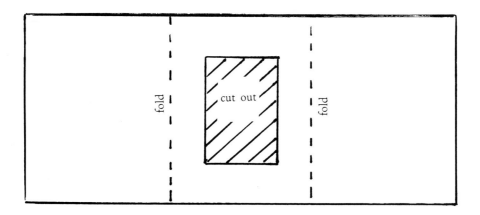

Swag of Flowers Card (23 × 15 cm)

This is a card for a special occasion.

Embroidered on a linen and polyester fabric, the flowers in the swag are spider's web roses in four colours, varying in size a little.

Yellow daisies are worked in perle cotton No. 8 in detached chain with a straight stitch inside.

The trumpet flowers are in buttonhole circles and stem stitch, worked in one strand of stranded cotton.

French knots in perle cotton No. 5 fill small spaces, and the leaves are worked with two strands of stranded cotton in two colours, using detached chains with a straight stitch inside.

The bow, in satin ribbon, was tied, then arranged and pinned to the fabric, then sewn.

The card was cut from Ingres paper, as in the instructions for the Knot Flower Cards, and the border drawn with a gold ballpoint pen and a green felt pen.

Key

French knots

detached chains

detached chain

stem stitch

buttonholed circle

spider's web

Wild Roses Card

(16 × 10 cm)

On a background of calico.

The three large roses are worked with five petals each, two roses in silk ribbon and one in polyester satin ribbon. (See Wild Rose on page 29.)

The large roses are surrounded by small roses, French knots and groups of detached chain stitches in 4 mm cream silk ribbon.

Yellow French knots in four strands of stranded cotton form the centres of the roses.

Bowl of Flowers Card

(16 × 10 cm)

Worked on a velveteen background, the flowers include spider's web roses in shaded knitting ribbon, violets in two shades of 4 mm silk ribbon, small rosebuds in satin ribbon, and groups of French knots in silk and satin ribbons.

The feathery foliage is in groups of fly stitches worked in silk thread.

The bowl is worked in rows of stem stitch in two strands of stranded cotton, with a few lines in a shiny rayon machine thread.

GIFTS

Chatelaine

A chatelaine, worn around the neck while sewing, is a very special gift for someone who enjoys needlework. The two large hearts form needlecase and pincushion; the small one holds a thimble.

You will need
card (or plastic from an icecream container)
fabric (silk is nice for a special gift)
2 m of 3 mm satin ribbon in two shades
2 m of 3 mm soft ribbon in a toning shade
perle cotton Nos. 5 and 8
stranded cotton in a contrast colour
thin wadding
flannel
1.5 m of 10 mm floral ribbon to tone with the
    embroidery
1.5 m of 10 mm plain ribbon to tone with the
    floral ribbon
sewing cotton to match the fabric
fabric glue
selection of needles
pearl or glass-headed pins
thimble
embroidery scissors

Method
1. Cut out six large hearts in fabric, as in the diagram, allowing 1 cm turning all round.
2. Embroider the design on two hearts, taking care to centre the design. Attach heart shaped pieces of flannel, slightly smaller than the large heart, to two other hearts.
3. Cut four smaller fabric hearts, as in the diagram, allowing 1 cm turnings.
4. Embroider one.
5. Cut six large hearts and four smaller ones from card or plastic, and seven large and two small from thin wadding.
6. Lightly glue the wadding to the plastic or card hearts.
7. Cover the wadding with the fabric, carefully making small cuts in the curves so that the edges fold over the edges of the card or plastic.
8. Glue the fabric to the back only. Use the minimum amount of a good fabric glue and apply it to the back of the card or plastic with a large darning needle.

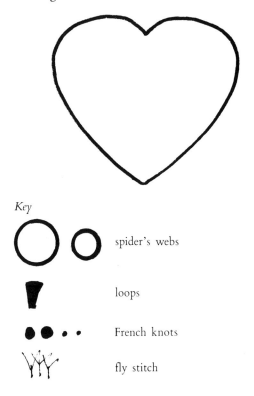

Key

◯ ◯   spider's webs

▼   loops

● ● • ·   French knots

Ⅶ Ⅶ   fly stitch

You should now have six large hearts (two embroidered, two with flannel, and two plain) and four small hearts, one embroidered and the others plain. There should be a heart in wadding left over.

9. Machine stitch the floral and plain ribbons together. This makes a strong, attractive ribbon on which to attach the hearts.

10. Glue one plain large heart 15 cm from one end of the floral ribbon, and one 30 cm from the other end.

11. Glue one small plain heart over the 15 cm end.

12. Place the spare wadding heart, trimmed slightly, on one of the plain hearts. Cover it with an embroidered heart and ladder stitch together. This is the pincushion and should have pins stuck round it.

13. Glue short lengths of 10 mm ribbon to the point of the other plain large heart and embroidered large heart. This forms a hinge for the needlecase.

14. Glue a loop of 3 mm satin ribbon to the centre top of the embroidered heart.

15. Ladder stitch the two hearts with flannel to these two hearts.

16. Cover a button with a circle of fabric and work a spider's web rose on it; sew the button to the floral ribbon just above the needlecase, so that the needlecase can be closed by the ribbon loop over the button.

17. Glue a small length of ribbon to the small embroidered heart. It should be long enough to fit over the thimble which is held in by it.

18. Sew the other two plain hearts to these with ladder stitch, then ladder stitch the two lined halves together. Sew a press fastener to the ribbon tab and to the ribbon above the heart.

19. Pass the 30 cm end of floral ribbon through the handles of a pair of embroidery scissors and sew the end 11.5 cm up the ribbon. The scissors should be able to be opened easily.

20. Add a selection of needles to the flannel in the needlecase and the chatelaine is finished.

Round Box

You will need
0.5 m of velvet or velveteen
1 m of 8 mm satin ribbon in deep pink
0.5 m of 8 mm satin ribbon in light red
sewing cotton in colours to match the ribbons
1 m each of 3 mm satin ribbon in red, orange and
 deep pink
1 m of 3 mm satin ribbon in pink
2 m silk or soft polyester ribbon in green
perle cotton in red and two shades of pink
stranded cotton in jacaranda blue
250 g tin, empty and clean, with cut off lid
 (salmon tins are ideal)
felt or flannel 28 × 4 cm
firm lightweight cardboard
dacron wadding
fabric glue

Method
1. Cut a piece of velvet or velveteen about 16 cm square. Mark the centre with a tacking stitch, and tack a circle around it the size of the design.
2. Make one folded rose in the 8 mm red satin ribbon and three in the 8 mm pink satin ribbon.
3. Sew these to the centre of the design as shown in the diagram.
4. Work French knots, in red, pink and orange satin ribbon, densely around the roses.
5. Add a few knots in jacaranda blue stranded cotton, using it double (12 strands)
6. Work spider's webs in red perle cotton, then groups of detached chains, working two chains one inside the other for each petal.

7. Spider's webs in pink perle cotton are worked next, then pairs of twisted chains in 3 mm pink satin ribbon.
8. Add groups of French knots in red and pink perle cotton to fill out the circular design, then work groups of three straight stitches in green silk or soft polyester ribbon.

To make up
1. Glue a strip of felt or flannel to the side of the tin, between the top and bottom ridges. Leave a gap of about 1.5 cm at the seam of the tin. This is to accommodate the seam in the fabric covering.
2. Measure the circumference of the tin over the felt, and add 3 cm. Measure the depth of the tin, double it and add 4 cm. Cut a piece of velvet or velveteen on the cross or bias to these measurements.
3. Seam the velvet, taking in a little more seam in just under half the seam length. This wider seam will be *inside* the tin.
4. Turn right side out, flatten seam and ease over the tin, with the seam over the gap in the felt, and the narrower part of the seam to the outside of the tin. Leave 3 cm of fabric extending over the base of the tin. Run a little fabric glue around the ridge on the base of the tin. Work a running stitch in firm thread around the edge of the fabric at the base of the tin and gather until it fits firmly over the base of the tin. Press the fabric into the glue around the ridge.

Run a little glue around the inside join at the base of the tin, being careful not to get too much glue on the tin.

Put a little glue on the inside seam of the tin. Turn the excess fabric over to the inside of the tin, stretching it slightly, and press into the glue at the base of the tin. Work around the inside of the tin a little at a time. It takes practice to get a really neat finish with no wrinkles.

5. Cut a circle of fabric 2 cm wider all round than the tin lid. Gather it over the lid with firm thread, then glue it to the base of the tin and put a weight on it for a while.

6. Cut a circle of lightweight cardboard to fit easily into the covered tin. Lightly glue a circle of dacron wadding to the cardboard then cover with a circle of fabric gathered over it. This should fit into the tin very snugly, and does not really need to be glued in.

7. Cut a circle of cardboard for the lid, 1 cm wider in diameter than the covered tin. Glue a piece of dacron wadding the same size to the cardboard. Cut the embroidered fabric 2 cm wider all round than the cardboard, taking care to centre the embroidery. Gather over the padded cardboard with a firm thread, and pull tight, so that the fabric is stretched firmly over the lid.

8. Cut a circle of thin cardboard to fit easily into the tin, and cover this with fabric, gathering it over the cardboard. Carefully glue this to the inside of the lid. Always put the glue on the lining, never the lid. Press together firmly, then lay in the top of the tin with the top of the lid to the inside of the tin and put a weight on the lining for a short while.

The lining of the lid should fit snugly into the tin and keep the lid on.

Key

twisted chain

detached chain

straight stitch

French knot

spider's web

folded rose

Ribbon Vine Design

This design is suitable for blouses and lingerie. The section illustrated can be repeated and used horizontally or vertically.

Requirements are given for the stocking bag illustrated, which is worked on synthetic georgette. Silk or any fine fabric could be substituted.

If you are using the design on clothing, remember the hints on page 14.

You will need
fabric 70 × 54 cm
0.5 m of 5 mm soft polyester ribbon to tone with the fabric
2.5 m of 3 mm satin ribbon in a lighter tone
perle cotton No. 8 to match the ribbons
stranded cotton to match the ribbons
2 m each of 3 mm satin ribbon in two colours contrasting with the fabric
perle cotton No. 8 in one of these colours
sewing thread to match the fabric
2 large beads with large holes (optional)

Method
1. Mark the centre of the fabric, lengthwise and across the width, with a line of basting.
2. On one section transfer the design to the fabric so that the top of the design is 18 cm from the top edge (see the section on transferring designs).
3. Tack the 5 mm ribbon to the appropriate line of the design, being very careful to get a smoothly curved line.
4. Attach the ribbon to the fabric with French knots in four strands of stranded cotton.
5. Baste two lines of satin ribbon and attach them with herringbone stitch over the ribbon, using one strand of stranded cotton.
6. Work whipped chain over the other two lines in perle cotton No. 8.
7. Work French knots in two colours of 3 mm satin ribbon in groups. Use more of one colour than the other. Work French knots in perle cotton No. 8 among the ribbon knots to make a dense bunch.
8. Using three strands of stranded cotton work groups of double detached chain stitches, one inside the other, at the end of the clusters of knots.

To make up
1. Fold the fabric in half lengthwise, right sides together.
2. Machine stitch a 1 cm seam along the raw edges, leaving a 1 cm gap 10 cm from each end.
3. Turn to the right side and press, with the embroidery face down on a well padded surface.
4. Turn in 1 cm at the top and bottom edges, press, then slip stitch together.
5. Machine stitch a 1 cm casing 10 cm from each end.
6. Fold in half and slip stitch the sides together up to the casing.
7. Cut the remaining 3 mm ribbons into approximately 50 cm lengths and thread the same number of pieces through each casing.
8. Knot the ribbons together just outside the casing. A large bead can be threaded onto the ribbons before knotting.

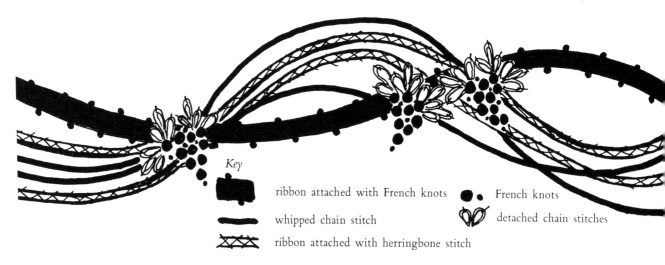

Key

◼ ribbon attached with French knots   ●• French knots

— whipped chain stitch   detached chain stitches

XXX ribbon attached with herringbone stitch

Spectacle Cleaner

You will need
fabric 18 × 15 cm approx.
chamois leather 16 × 7 cm approx.
plastic from icecream carton, 15 × 12 cm approx.
0.5 m of 5 mm satin ribbon
1 m each of two colours in 3 mm silk or soft
    polyester ribbon
stranded cotton in three shades
0.5 m of 1 cm satin or nylon ribbon
large bead with a large hole

Method
1. Cut out plastic, fabric and chamois leather according to the pattern.
2. Work embroidery on one half of one piece of fabric, starting with the spider's web in 5 mm satin ribbon, then irises in silk or polyester ribbon. The small flowers are next, also in silk ribbon with French knots in the centre. The French knots and long-tailed French knots are worked last, in three strands of stranded cotton.
3. Place one piece of plastic in the centre of the reverse side of the embroidered fabric. Run a gathering thread around the curved part of the shape, and pull up till the fabric fits over the plastic.
4. Lace across the back from side to side until the fabric is taut around the plastic.
5. Fold remaining half of the fabric over the reverse side, turn under and hem neatly just inside the edge of the shape.
6. Repeat steps 3 to 5 with the other piece of fabric.
7. Sew the two halves together, starting 0.5 mm from centre top and using a slanting stitch in three strands of stranded cotton to match the fabric. On reaching the lower edge stitch back over the stitches to form a cross stitch. Repeat on the other side.
8. Thread the 1 cm ribbon through the centre of the chamois leather and, using a long darning needle, through the hole in the top of the case.
9. Thread both ends of ribbon through a bead and tie a knot behind it. The ribbon should extend about 8 cm, plus bead, from the top of the case when the chamois leather is pulled inside it.

This makes a very attractive and useful gift for anyone who wears glasses. It is small enough to be carried in purse or pocket.

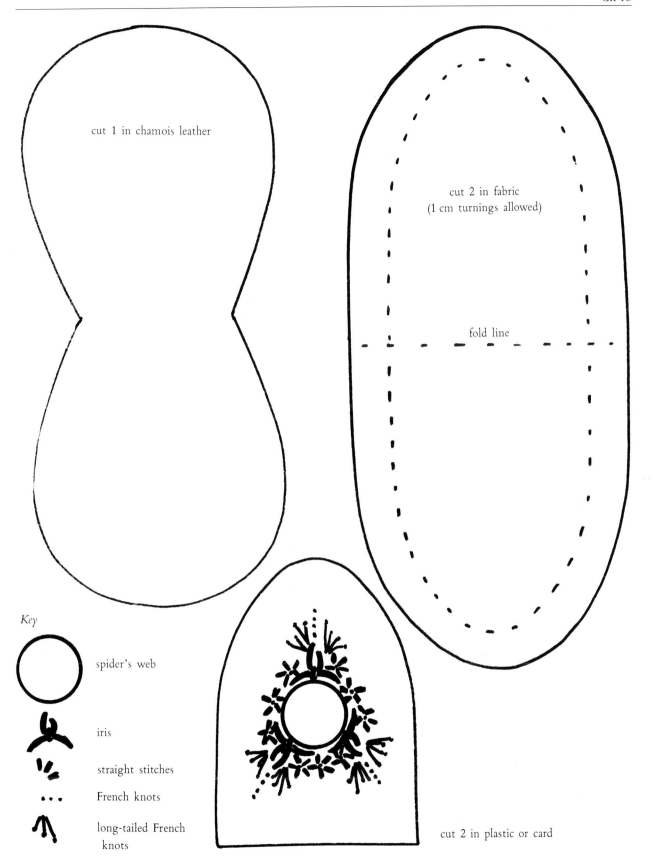

cut 1 in chamois leather

cut 2 in fabric
(1 cm turnings allowed)

fold line

Key

spider's web

iris

straight stitches

French knots

long-tailed French
knots

cut 2 in plastic or card

Cosmetic Bag, Tissue Holder and Comb Case

You will need
velveteen 45 × 35 cm
interfacing 35 cm square
lining 70 × 35 cm
1 m of 7 mm wide silk ribbon
2 m each of 4 mm silk ribbon in two colours
1.5 m of 3 mm satin ribbon
perle cotton No. 5 in three colours
perle cotton No. 5 in a yellow to tone with the
    other colours
stranded cotton
(the colours in the illustration are a blend of close
    colours plus a soft yellow)
    The comb case and tissue holder should fit into
the cosmetic bag.

Method
1. From the velveteen cut a piece 32 × 19 cm.
2. With a basting thread mark where the three
wild roses will be, 5 cm from the edge of the
velveteen. Start with these flowers, working five
petals. Catch the underside of the loops down with
a small stitch. Work French knots at the centres.
3. Work a group of three detached chains in silk
ribbon at each side of the central flower.
4. Then work the spider's web roses in silk ribbon
and satin ribbon.
5. The bullion knot daisies are next, with a French
knot at the centre.
6. Groups of three French knots fill spaces, using
perle cotton No. 5 in three colours.
7. Lastly, add groups of fly stitches in one strand
of stranded cotton.
8. Cut pieces of velveteen 20 × 12 cm for the
tissue holder and 10 × 15 cm for the comb case.
9. Work the design similarly to the cosmetic bag.

To make up
1. Round off the corners on the embroidered end
of the cosmetic bag.
2. Cut a piece of lining the same size and a piece
of interfacing 1 cm smaller all round.
3. Fold the edge of the velveteen over the
interfacing and baste, taking care not to sew
through to the right side. On the curved edge it
is easier to run a gathering thread along the edge,
and pull up and ease the gathers to fit over the
interfacing before basting.
4. Cut a piece of lining 32 × 19 cm. Cut another
piece of lining 22 × 17 cm, fold in half on the
22 cm side and press so that the piece measures
11 × 17 cm. Fold under 1 cm of the edge opposite
the fold and press.
5. Place the folded piece on the lining one-third
of the way from top and lower edge and pin in
place.
6. Machine stitch along the turned-under edge,
then machine stitch a line 4 cm from the side, from
the folded edge to the end of the added piece. This
pocket will accommodate a compact and lipstick.
7. Pin the lining and pocket over the cosmetic bag,
turning in at the edges, and hand sew in place.
8. Turn up the lower edge of the lined bag to cover
the pocket, and neatly oversew the sides with
matching thread.
9. The tissue holder is constructed similarly, the
velveteen folded over the interfacing, and the lining
hand sewn to it.
10. Cut velveteen and lining 14 × 23 cm, then
bring the two ends together and centre them on
one half of the tissue holder.
11. Hand sew the sides with small overcast stitches.
12. Make up the comb case by the same method.
Cut velveteen and lining 15 × 11 cm, then fold
in half and overcast the side and lower edge.

1. Cosmetic bag

Key

	fly stitches
	bullion knots
	French knots
	chain stitch
	loops
	spider's web

2. Tissue holder

3. Comb case

Hydrangea Box Top

This design could be used on clothing or an evening bag as well, as the flowers can be extended to fill any shape.

Each flower is composed of four petals, worked here in shaded knitting ribbon, in two straight stitches almost on top of one another for each petal.

The petal is outlined with four iridescent bugle beads, with a sequin and a round bead to form the centre of the flower.

Instead of knitting ribbon, several shades of 4 mm silk ribbon could be used.

The stitches are always left rather loose, but the right tension comes with experience.

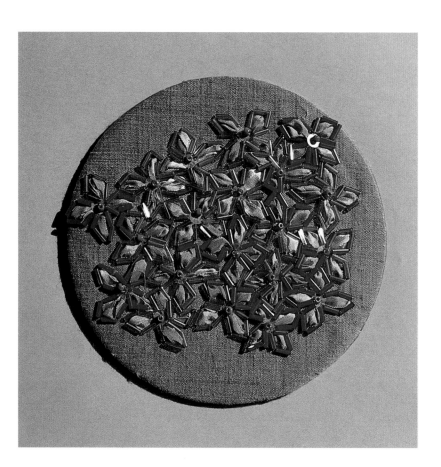

Blue and Green Box Top

This design is embroidered on a dark blue taffeta, and worked in a frame.

The circular flower forms are spider's webs in silk and polyester ribbons. Each is surrounded by a ring of beads. These were strung on a thread first, and then couched between every second bead to form the ring.

The stems are very long bugle beads in royal blue and turquoise.

Rings of buttonhole stitch in royal blue perle cotton No. 5 are worked on top of the other circles, with a scattering of small royal blue beads around and above them, with a few green beads among them.

This design would also be suitable for an evening bag, or could be extended for a border design for clothing.

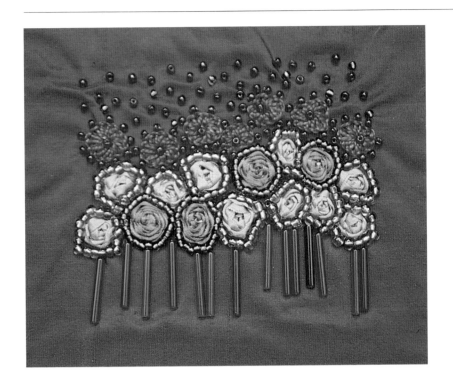

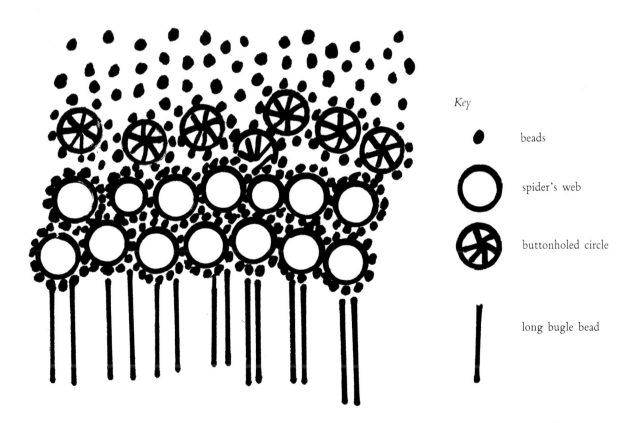

Key

● beads

○ spider's web

✴ buttonholed circle

| long bugle bead

Floral Spray Box Top

This design would fit into a wooden box with a recessed lid. Many embroidery and craft shops carry such boxes, in assorted sizes. The fabric used in the illustrated embroidery is shot silk. The design size of 10 × 5 cm will fit a recess 12 × 7 cm.

You will need
fabric the size of the box lid or recess, plus 2 cm all round
1 m shaded knitting ribbon, or two shades of 4 mm silk ribbon
0.5 m each of 4 mm satin ribbon in two colours

0.5 m of 2 mm silk ribbon
stranded cotton in a green to tone with the other
  colours
small quantity of seed beads in the main colour

Method
1. Start with the three central roses, which are
worked in spider's webs, the centre rose shaded
and the two either side in satin ribbon.
2. Next work the two daisies in detached chains
in 2 mm silk ribbon.
3. The groups of three French knots in satin ribbon
follow.
4. Then work three stalks from the end of the
flower spray, using stem stitch in two strands of
stranded cotton. These stalks measure approximately 2 cm from the central area and 1.2 cm at
each side.
5. At the ends of the stalks work rosebuds in two
straight stitches, one over the other, in either the
shaded ribbon or the two shades of silk ribbon.
Add straight stitches in two strands of stranded

cotton at each side and on the centre of each bud,
and at the top of the bud (see rosebuds on page 29).
6. Next work a group of detached chain stitches
at the base of the stalks, in the same stranded
cotton.
7. Then work the other groups of leaves in
detached chain stitches.
8. The groups of beads are added last, starting with
three beads at the base of the group, then two,
then three single beads.

To make up
1. Cut a piece of thin cardboard to fit easily into
the recess. Allow for the fabric to cover it, but
it must be a very neat fit. Glue a piece of thin
wadding to the cardboard—a dab of glue at each
corner is enough.
2. Cover the padded cardboard with the
embroidery and glue to the back of the cardboard
with fabric glue. Make sure the embroidery is
centred and taut.
3. Glue into the recess on the box.

Key

 seed beads

 straight stitches

 stem stitch

 French knot

 detached chains

 spider's web

Tissue Holder

The tissue holder is for purse-size packets of tissues. It is best made in a firm fabric, which should be washable.

The design is simple to work as it consists of chain stitch and French knots only.

You will need
fabric 30 × 14 cm
1 m each of 3 mm satin ribbon and two shades of silk or soft polyester ribbon
shiny thread or stranded cotton to tone with the ribbons
stranded cotton in a contrast colour
sewing cotton to match the fabric

Method
1. Fold the piece of fabric in half, then fold again, so that the first fold lies on the stitching line at the raw edge. Press the fold firmly. If the fabric is springy, baste a line on the fold. The embroidery is worked between the centre fold and the two outer folds and should be approximately 1.5 cm from the outer fold.
2. Work the two lines of embroidery, starting with the satin ribbon, then the silk ribbons, followed by chain stitch in a shiny thread, and the French knots. The leaf design is in opposite directions each side of the opening of the tissue holder.
3. Seam the two raw edges, right sides together. Press seam open.
4. Turn to the right side and fold in and press the side edges. The seam should lie in the centre on the reverse side to the embroidery.
5. With the embroidery to the inside, fold the edges to the centre. They should just meet.
6. Stitch across the ends.
7. Turn to the right side and press carefully, with the embroidery face down.
8. Stitch each side of the opening together with a few neat stitches, and insert tissues.

Key

chain stitches

French knots

INDEX